This is a book to be read outside –
may it go waterlogged, sun-buckled and wind-chapped.

LYNNE ROPER

Wild Woman Swimming

A Journal of West Country Waters

EDITED BY TANYA SHADRICK

THE SELKIE *PRESS*

First published in Great Britain in 2018
Second edition published in August 2018

The Selkie Press
12 Bradford Road
Lewes
East Sussex
BN7 1RB

www.selkiepress.com

Printed and bound by Clays Ltd, Elcograf S.p.A.

A catalogue record for this book is available from the British Library

ISBN 978 1 5272 2198 7

THE **SELKIE** *PRESS*

*'From the outer edge of your circles of loved ones
know I'll keep my promise to you.'*

Tanya Shadrick to Lynne Roper (August 2016)

CONTENTS

PREFACE

I first saw Lynne Roper in a video made for *The Guardian*: she was encouraging a novice into the waters of the River Dart with quintessential enthusiasm. I'd already heard of her; she was at the centre of a mandala of connections. I remember watching the video and understanding why so many would want her friendship. She was lively, smart and articulate, with an unhurried charm that was utterly appealing. She had the qualities of a favoured teacher, aunt, sister, and a glimmer of fun in her eyes. I watched the video again recently in the hope I could still catch something of her essence, and there it was, in the moment when she did a joyful leap into 9-degree water with a loud exclamation of pleasure. There was Lynne.

Conjuring someone up on screen even when they are dead is something my generation is still getting used to; it can feel like emotional trickery. We are much more accustomed to a legacy of words, and the thing that has surprised me about Lynne's words is just how present she is in them. Her essence is here, you can catch it on every page, hear her voice. That's such a cliché, isn't it, the 'writer's voice'. But it's here, revealing her as successfully as any video.

If Lynne's death was deeply untimely, this book is certainly not. We're in the middle of a publishing wave – yes, let's call it that – of writing about water, particularly but not exclusively from women. Books where swimming has been both subject and metaphor. I will declare my hand: I am one of those women writers. In *Swell, A Waterbiography*, I included a chapter on 'why women swim', hoping that if I asked enough women I might divine one single unifying answer, a meaning-of-life type revelation (spoiler: there isn't one answer. We swim for all manner of reasons.) I wanted Lynne in that chapter because she was such a vital presence in the outdoor swimming community. It's not that she had a unique view; the peace she found in the water was a common thread. What she had was a unique talent to draw everything in just a few words. To communicate with humility – this is the writer's dream. To write of friendship, nature, climate, geography, bodies, cake, swimming, all of it, with understated charisma and humour.

New traditions are being forged; new genres nudged into being. Spaces carved for women to write about what they feel and what they know. Put simply: some of us have 'found' ourselves in the water and shared that in our writing. I don't know if Lynne 'found' herself, or was ever lost, but even the strongest, most capable amongst us can relish the opportunity for self-reflection that comes from being in water; Lynne certainly articulated how much more 'herself' she felt, afloat. There are parts of Lynne's experiences that people might not get – her enduring love of the cold, obstinate sea, for instance. But not everything has to be understood. Sometimes it can just be incredible, evocative, or plain old funny.

Lynne called herself a 'wild woman', and this book honours that. Wild women don't do what they're told. They're difficult, they don't follow social niceties and sometimes they don't even brush their hair. Wild women are the corrupting influences in folk tales, the spell weavers, the kidnappers, the bad cooks. Wild women are the ones who laugh the loudest, wink and whistle, sneak off and skinny-dip, who take pleasure in the simplest of things, who ask very little of the world yet give a whole lot in return.

Who wouldn't want to be a wild woman?

JENNY LANDRETH
Author of *Swell: A Waterbiography*

INTRODUCTION

I first met Lynne in December 2011 when we explored a famous local rock arch near Torquay called London Bridge. Inside its cave, we shrieked and whooped as the swell bounced us up and down, and I felt an instant connection with this woman who was to become a great friend and fellow adventurer. On that occasion I also met several other people who were to become close companions (and fellow regulars in Lynne's swim diaries), including Queenie, Jonathan – known as JJ – Steph, and Allan. We had a few precious years wild swimming together, before Jonathan died in 2013, followed by Lynne in 2016. The day when we all met for the first time – described so vividly by Lynne in her diaries – has great poignancy for me.

As Lynne was dying of a brain tumour in 2016, I sat in the hospital waiting-room with her mother Jenny, who told me in a way Lynne's impending death was not a surprise. 'She always grabbed life with both hands, ever since she was a small girl. It was as though she somehow knew she had to make the most of every moment; that she would not have a long life.'

And that sums up Lynne so well: She relished every instant. Her writing demonstrates her fierce intelligence, humour, dry wit, and passionate engagement with the world. Her descriptions of experiences in the wild waters of Devon reveal her gloriously imaginative sensibility. She had an ability not only to evoke the moment but to give it context, and link it to other areas of life – the common joys, mundanities and heartbreak we all experience.

Lynne was a Devonian through and through. Born in Tiverton, she then spent some of her childhood by the sea in Watcombe, where her father had been posted as a police officer. She adored Devon but above all loved Dartmoor, where she lived for the last part of her life in a small miner's cottage at Mary Tavy, which she decorated in various combinations of bright pink and turquoise complete with a mermaid mosaic on the bathroom wall she created herself. ('I don't do beige', she declared proudly on her Airbnb listing.)

A voracious reader, her knowledge of Dartmoor was considerable. She introduced me to the book *High Dartmoor* by Eric Hemery which – published in 1983 – was one of the more recent pieces of great writing about the moor. Lynne frequently uses the name 'Double Dart' in her diaries to refer to the River Dart; this was a name used by Hemery to describe the stretch of the river downstream of Dartmeet, where the East and West Dart rivers converge to form the Dart. Very few people refer to the Double Dart these days, but Lynne's use of the name shows her love for Hemery's scholarly precision.

I remember walking along the Dart with her one day and remarking on the strange, almost human, wailing sound coming from the gorge. She told me about the legend of Jan Coo, a farm hand who lived at Rowbrook Farm, high above the remotest part of the gorge in between Dartmeet and New Bridge. Jan kept running down to the river, thinking someone was calling him. Each time he would come back, confused and disappointed there was nobody there. The final time he responded to the call he never returned. There was a rumour the pixies had taken him. Lynne told me this related to another legend, that every year the Dart takes a life: 'Dart, Dart, cruel Dart, every year thou claim'st a heart.'

I've lost count of the many happy times in and by the Dart. Sitting in Horseshoe Falls, braced against the pounding water and putting our faces in, to be kissed by a million bubbles. Jumping in off Black Rock and swirling around in the eddy. Lynne's leggy labradoodle, Honey, stealing cakes at post-swim picnics. And numerous attempts at moonlit dips, which Lynne called 'Moon Gazey swims'. Here's what she wrote about them:

> We call them Moon Gazey swims after moon gazey hares,
> who sit mesmerised by the full moon. There's also the
> famous Star Gazey Pie, traditional in Cornwall where
> the heads of the pilchards rise above the pastry, like wild
> swimmers scoffing their way out of a giant cake. Being in
> Devon, many of our Moon Gazey swims involve mist, rain
> and thick cloud. It doesn't usually stop us.

Lynne's creative mind was always on the go, her imagination conjuring up swims which became original, transformative experiences. There were the Moon Gazey swims, usually in the sea, but many others too. A Midsummer night's swim at Spitchwick on the Dart was one I wasn't lucky enough to attend but read about afterwards. Everyone gathered at dusk, festooned with greenery and wearing flowery headdresses, and there was a bizarre encounter with the police who were following up reports of an illegal rave. Then there was the famous 'umbrella swim', where everyone floated down the Avon Estuary to Bantham on the outgoing tide, holding wildly-decorated brollies above their heads.

Great friendships were made on all these many and varied swims. Lynne had a gift for bringing people together and nurturing those who were less confident. We explored all over Dartmoor and along the South Devon coast, a motley band of people from varying backgrounds who might never have met were it not for our shared love of swimming outdoors. Somehow, imperceptibly, our bond became about much more than just sharing an activity. When Jackie told us she was getting married to Gordon after more than twenty years together, we all got knitting to create a wedding blanket for her. When another friend, Linda, suffered a catastrophic illness, we did the same. And when Lynne was dying, we went to work once more.

Community is an overused word, but we do have a wonderfully close and vibrant wild swimming community here in Devon, and much of that is down to Lynne. Although we miss her dreadfully, we are fortunate to have not only amazing memories but her extraordinary diaries. In the following pages you will read compelling accounts of swims all over Devon, from the romantic to the ridiculous, and from the hilarious to the haphazard; Lynne's intelligent, articulate and imaginative voice lives on in her words on the page.

Thank you Lynne, for all the memories. The water, whether sea, lake or river, will always take me back to you. It is formless, vast and never-ending; like infinity, frightening and reassuring at the same time. I think of you slipping into the Dart, and I smile.

SOPHIE PIERCE
Author of *Wild Swimming Walks: Dartmoor and South Devon* and *Beyond the Beach: The Secret Wild Swims of Torbay*

LYNNE ROPER

Wild Woman Swimming

A Journal of West Country Waters

2 0 1 1

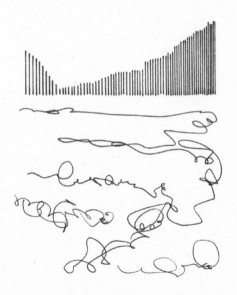

SHARRAH

8 October

~

We formed Devon Wild Swimmers this spring and have yet to arrange a moonlight swim where the moon actually appears through the mizzle. But one of the universal traits of wild swimmers is the refusal to be deterred by poor weather.

The Dart is known as a 'flashy' river however, and it's impossible to swim there if the water is too high. A pessimistic weather forecast had me worrying it would be too dangerous, so the swim was cancelled. Dan the Weather Man (a fellow wild swimmer) then assured us – under threat of being barbecued if he was wrong – that this side of the moor would be okay. So it was that six humans and two dogs met at New Bridge on the Double Dart river on an overcast Saturday evening, in order to walk up to Sharrah Pool for a swim.

We wandered in the Dartmoor dusk through the ancient woodlands of the Dart valley carrying our swimming gear. The river was up slightly, and a cool 12 degrees. We were cocooned by the woodland, enveloped in her damp, earthy smell, and the sound of the river which ebbed and flowed according to the distance of the track from her banks. The light was fading properly as we arrived at the stile near Sharrah, where we had a sudden, brief glimpse of the moon dribbling silvery light through the clouds, silhouetting the gnarly branches and remaining leaves of the sessile oaks and beech trees. From there we made our way down through the glade to the flattish rocks on the riverbank, assailed by the roar and fizzing energy from the upper waterfall.

After a prolonged struggle with a damp wetsuit and new booties I was finally able to get in, desperate for the feel of chill, silky water and the refreshing taste of peat. The water seeped into my wetsuit and chilled me beautifully, so I struck out in breaststroke upstream towards the falls, duck-diving under the water to cool my sweaty face and de-midge my hair.

Behind the shadow of the boulder in the centre of the river is a still pathway where you can swim unimpeded. We all met at this rock and climbed around it to the edge of the rapid that runs from the falls down the far, steep granite bank to the bottom end of the pool. Standing on a submerged ledge, we flung ourselves downstream into the current which was visible as creamy, beery foam surging past. The ride through the dark and the spray was exhilarating, our bodies being gathered up in the rapid as the river took control.

If quick, we could escape from the rapid on the far side and climb onto the rocks. I did this, then watched as my friends' white faces materialised from the dark and shot past me like meteorites. Then I jumped back in to the space-black water, hearing the whoosh as I plunged down, down, down, waiting in the dark to feel my feet touch the bottom before bouncing back up, gasping.

We changed on the bank, happy and laughing and not too cold at all. On the walk back it was completely dark, so we used head-torches. The muddy, rocky path was splattered with autumn leaves. Some had fallen with their underneath upwards and, sprinkled with drizzle droplets, they glowed in the torchlight. Fungus became more visible on crumbling trees, dense and white. The sounds of the river came and went.

The sky began to clear, with cirrus cloud back-lit by the moon and the odd glimmer from a star. A barn owl screeched like a ghost in the woods.

LOOE
9 October

~

I met up with Cornwall Wild Swimmers this morning at low tide for a swim around Looe Island.

I make that sound simple. Actually, I couldn't find them to start with, and my request for directions to the beach from a local with a Cockney accent was met with the response: 'At the end of the river.'

When I did arrive, the sea was flat and pale turquoise and the sky clear. In we went, and away we swam – using front crawl, on account of my companions being the marine equivalent of racing snakes.

Forging through the salty water, I flew over kelp beds, ginger-brown, luscious, and splodged with some unidentified white stuff that resembled seagull shit. Popping my head up for a moment, I floated alongside cormorants that perched – black Brylcream boys – on part of the reef that pokes above the surface.

Then, suddenly, I became entangled in a patch of weed that snaked around my arms and legs like Medusa's hair. Swallowing a good quart of water, with its pooey, seaweedy scent, I managed to disentangle myself. Slipping through in breaststroke, I found a channel through the weed and sped up again, noticing the distant ripples in the sandy bottom. Here I faced beautiful, deep-red weeds, suspended upright in the water, with arching fronds that each ended in a pom-pom like a poodle's tail.

As we left the shelter of the bay, a squall blew up and we were met with a suddenly frisky wind and speeding wavelets that slapped our faces like angry strumpets. We pushed through and

7

hit another kelp-field. Then, reaching the island, a large sign became visible: NO LANDING. Richard and Pauline ignored this advice.

Maggie and I decided to return to the shore. We were now being pulled parallel to it and tossed around on wavelets hitting us side-on. I really enjoy this kind of tussle with the elements, so continued to breathe on the downwind side. But then I noticed how the lovely poodle-tail weeds were being pushed out horizontally by the current, and realised what we were up against.

Maggie, who is rather slender for a wild swimmer, was worried about the cold and current both, so asked me to keep a close eye out for her... then immediately took off at the kind of speed that would give Becky Adlington a swim for her money. Floundering along, rolling from side-to-side in the chop, I stopped occasionally to keep my promise. I thought I caught sight of Maggie's red hat on the horizon once or twice, but it could have been a buoy. Luckily, she made it back to shore in one piece, and considerably ahead of me.

I always feel as though I've had six pints of scrumpy when I stand up to wade in from the sea. I've a vision in my head of looking like Ursula Andress, while actually resembling in my shiny, black wetsuit a pissed masochist who's seen better days. But it's how you feel that counts, and I felt great.

SPITCHWICK
14 October
~

Honey and I popped over to Spitchwick this morning. It's a warmish autumn day, with a slightly chill breeze. There's still some heat in the sun which pops out occasionally from behind puffy, greying clouds illuminating the ponies grazing on the common by the river. We can smell their gorgeous, horsey scent and, in Honey's case, the mouth-watering whiff of tottering heaps of steaming dung.

It's 11 degrees in the water today, so I decide on a wetsuit because I want to swim for at least thirty minutes. As I enter the river down the stone 'steps', I notice a dipper who performs his jerky little dance from a rock by the island before bobbing under the water, then zipping away downstream. His cream bib makes his low-level flight visible for a little while. Honey potters around in the shallows, then swims across and back. I can hear her breathing in little puffs as she passes.

The water today is mirror-black on the far side. The leaves on the trees behind are turning and their full height is reflected as though soaked into the water. On the near side I can see coppery patches here and there, but for the most part the gravelly bottom has been obliterated by huge drifts of autumn leaves and twiggy debris from last month's stormy weather. The leaves blacken as they decompose, and the newer ones – orange, greeny-yellow and tan – glow randomly through the peaty water like jewels, flashing in the current. When I step in, I sink to my ankles in the spongy layer then slide to the side as my foot hits a hidden rock. It's safer to just swim, so I leap forwards and plunge straight under before turning to head upstream against the current on the far side, where it's deep.

The water of the Double Dart smells and tastes of the moors: chill, fresh, pure and peaty. I swim in front crawl to warm up, and the water beneath me is black as night. Silver bubbles arc from my hands, which glow disembodied through the water in an eerie, copper light. Icy rivulets push through the neck of my suit and down my back like shivers from a ghost story. And then

9

it hits: full-on ice-cream head for the first time since the spring. I try to swim through but have to stop so I float on my back, arms outstretched, in a cross. The pain in my forehead subsides and I can hear only my amplified breathing in my submerged ears. Blue sky, clouds, oak trees, and the edge of a backlit cloud. I begin to turn in the current and stay there for a while, before swimming again. After the third go, the ice-cream head is no more so I carry on upstream, then back down at four times the pace, then float around until I start to feel cold again.

I can hear Honey growling and barking from the bank and stand up to watch her. Her hair is soaked and curling, and she's charging around the common in a zig-zag pattern with a stick in her mouth. Occasionally she tosses and catches the stick, arse and loopy tail waving, having a big, doggy laugh. I love that a wild swim affects my dog in the same way that it affects me, or maybe we're both just crazy bitches?

On the walk back, I notice that a crone of a crabapple tree, bearded with lichens, has shed her load of pale yellow fruit. We stop, and I pick them up in my towel, leaving the ones that lie in horseshit for Honey, who is partial to a windfall apple or ten. She tries one but declines the rest, possibly because they're a little sour, or because the horse poo is not fresh enough, like sour cream.

Gazing up at the tree, I see a sprinkling of crabapples still clinging to the branches and looking, against the greeny-grey lichen, like a fruity tiara on a tipsy granny at a barn dance. The music of the river fades as we walk away.

THURLESTONE ROCK
23 October

~

Thurlestone Rock, icon of the South Devon coast, sits around five hundred metres off shore at high tide, sturdy legs astride, and just begs to be swum through. It's near the end of a reef that runs perpendicular to the shore; the reef is legendary for its beautiful underwater garden of seaweeds and aquatic creatures. I'd not swum here before, and the 40 knot south-easterly whipping up the sea promised to make the swim slightly more sporting than we had expected it to be.

As we walked down the short track to the beach, my swim buddy JJ told us that on arrival he'd been immediately accosted by a local, who exclaimed at the perilous state of the sea and informed him that anyone attempting to swim would certainly be drowned and dashed onto the rocks. This was clearly an exaggeration, although we did have a chat before getting in about the best route to take and decided to stay on the lee of the reef, and to swim beyond the rock and around to the far side before deciding on whether to swim through.

The steeply-shelving beach means that the surf rolls almost to the shore before breaking directly downwards with great force. So, you have to run in between waves, and hope to be out beyond the breaking zone before one gets you and smashes you onto the shingle like a piece of kelp ripped from a rock. Unfortunately, a couple of our group got caught and found it a bit too heavy to carry on. I timed my entrance for the little gap between the breaking of one wave and the arrival of the next, diving forwards into the approaching breaker so I'd gone through just before it broke.

Once we were heading off-shore it became much easier to swim

11

through the rollers. You just go with them, breathe when you can, and try to stay in touch with a couple of other swimmers. As we neared the reef, I noticed that the swell had grown and was big enough intermittently to obscure the Thurlestone from view. I found it much harder to swim smoothly and was rolled almost onto my back a couple of times. I did the usual water-swallowing but managed not to inhale any for once. I looked up at the rock, and saw regular swimmer Maretta with her young daughter, who was out on her first wild swim and looking as though she was born in the sea, sliding through the swell like a little seal.

The sea was an opaque greeny-blue through my goggles as I swam, and when I stopped and looked at its surface it was the colour of pewter. The sun was low and partially covered by clouds; it emitted a chill light that glinted off the wavelets ahead. I swam out a little way past the rock, which was sideways on to me then, to take some photos. I tried to work out how high it is. It's probably only 30 feet or so above the sea, but somehow looks much larger. It's made up of two rock stacks that lean in towards each other and touch around fifteen feet above the sea. There is a fissure running vertically from the point where the leg stacks meet. The rock is dark and jagged with a texture like bark on an ancient oak, and its outline is broken further by the silhouetted sea birds that cling to its summit – cormorants and gulls with beaks pointing skywards.

I swam back to the other swimmers and looked over towards the hole that was just visible at an angle. The waves, some around six feet high, were smashing into the stack nearest the shore at an angle, splatting spume across the rough surface like whipped egg whites. The crazy angles of the sea made the arch look quite menacingly mad. Pauline told me they'd decided it was too dangerous to go through, so everyone began to swim off shore-wards down the side of the reef.

I watched the waves for a bit and looked behind to see how quickly they were coming. Some were smaller than others, and I began to wonder whether I could make it through, and, if not, whether I could push off the far side of the arch with my legs and escape a bashing that way. 'You're thinking of going through, aren't you?' said JJ. Hmmm, yes.

There was a quick discussion. We reckoned we could make it between waves. We were now pretty close, being pushed by the swell towards the rock. 'We're already committed, let's just body-surf through' said Pauline, and so we went for it. I swam towards the nearest offshore stack of the arch, so that if I was washed off course I might hit the gap. A wave came through and I put my head down and swam flat out through the hole, shooting out of the other side with a rush of adrenaline to find we'd made it: me, Pauline, JJ and Wee Man Martin, all laughing and shouting with the exhilaration.

I looked back and realised we were still very close to the rock, and that there was a huge wave approaching. It hit the arch and the small rock next to it, then surged and broke over the top. The water on this side, made more turbulent by its route through the stone, foamed and churned in sympathy with our little gang of excitable swimmers. We bobbed around for a bit, took a couple of quick snaps and swam bravely away towards the shore, over the reef.

Floating face down, I tried to see the reef garden, but the turbulent water made visibility poor. I glimpsed through the murky, pale turquoise water some pale grey rocks with swirling seaweed rooted firmly to them, but that was it garden-wise. But who could be disappointed after the fun of the swim and the crazy surf through the Thurlestone?

I managed to avoid being dumped by the surf at the shoreline, and ran for it over the shingle of small, smooth quartz pebbles to the beach. We were all high as teenagers at a rave.

'We'll have to swim it again to see the garden,' said Kirsty through a mouthful of mint tea and home-made biscuit. The Thurlestone squatted behind her in the distance, surrounded by silver sea.

SHARRAH

1 November

~

I drove across the moors through splatting showers, sunshine and rainbows. Heavy rain overnight had raised the river considerably. Foam billowed on ginger and dun water, and kayakers littered the surface by New Bridge. We walked up the track through squidgy mud and the scent of leaf mould, rendered speechless by a glade of zinging yellow leaves still clinging to the trees.

Sharrah appeared through the warm, woodland colours; black water speckled with white flotsam. Today the pool had lost her tranquility, and the surface was in a slow boil. Upstream towards the waterfall, the river surged, and spray misted the view. I swam towards the falls from the nearly submerged rocks, feet like ice. The cacophony of the cascade intensified and swirled around. The river fought me, forcing me backwards and so I switched from breaststroke to front crawl, puffing from the cold, and with an icy chill reaching my brain through my face. When I made it to the eddy, it was filled with turrets of beery foam like drifts of partially-thawed snow. I reached the central rock, grabbed it and then flung myself into the rapid, shooting downstream among strange little bergs formed from bubbles the size of my head.

14

As I swam, gold and orange leaves flashed past my hands like autumn fish.

FOGGINTOR
2 November
~

Mist is descending and the wind picking up as Honey and I walk along the bleak track to Foggintor Quarry. The approach looks like something from a post-apocalyptic movie in this grey November light. Most people imagine Dartmoor to be a wilderness, but it's a man-made landscape. The earth has been quarried and mined for millennia; Foggintor and neighbouring Swell Tor were hollowed out in the 18th and 19th centuries. Their granite now lives in the walls of Dartmoor prison and some other famous landmarks, including Nelson's Column.

As we draw alongside the quarry entrance we see a little vista opening up through the passageway to the centre of the tor. Juicy green turf, ivy-green mosses, and little ponds of lettuce-green weed entice us through to the pool. Sheer cliffs rise around fifty feet from the slaty water, which is being whipped into wavelets. From time to time, I watch the progress of a gust of wind as it agitates the surface causing a swirling, transient opacity. The smell of sheep wee fades.

I change in the chill wind, and swim towards the tiny islands. The water is cold and satiny. I pass over tumbled heaps of granite and occasionally scrape my hand or my knee; sometimes I notice them in time and bank like a low-flying jet-fighter negotiating a canyon. When I look up I see the cliffs begin to fade like ghosts into the mist.

I love being in the womb of what was once a tor; I think of how the heart was ripped from her, and how nature has mended her wounds with a skin of turf and moss. The spring has bled into her exposed core and filled it, making a place for animals and birds to drink and wash, and for me and Honey to swim.

SPITCHWICK
11 November

~

'There will be a passing band of heavy rain, which will have cleared by the time we get there,' said Dan the Fish, Weather Forecaster to the Stars. 'We might even see the moon'.

We were due to meet at 6.30pm for our Moon Gazey Swim on the Double Dart. At 5.40, at home in Mary Tavy, I heard – through the sound of the deluge hammering on my roof – a faint 'bong' from my laptop. It was a message from Dan: 'It will stop raining now. Right now. It is written in the stars. Mars has gone into retrograde and Pisces is rising.'

Despite Dan's assurances, several people managed to find suitable excuses. The hardy Torbay contingent were forced to turn back when Jackie's car broke down, Dangerous Malcolm was swept away on the pavement outside Jackie's house, and Queenie – heading for her first Double Dart swim – made it all the way to the wrong bridge.

Honey and I drove tentatively across the moors, our little Jimny vanishing under an occasional wave. The water on the road at Dunnabridge was two feet deep in places and heading straight downhill to the West Dart. But we made it through the rain, and arrived at New Bridge to see Martin, Marie and Helena sheltering in their car which bobbed around the car park like a fishing float. We waited for Dan. Finally, at 6.45, his red Volvo screamed up in a cloud of spray. The door opened. 'I told you it would stop raining!' he grinned, as it continued to fall.

We'd already checked the water level: way too high for a swim at Sharrah and rising fast, so we set off for Spitchwick.

We sprang straight in to chilly water, shrieking with the cold. The smell of peat and the distant roar of the cascade faded as I went under. Even here on the slow side of the pool the current pulled hard, and it took me several minutes to get upstream in front crawl. Swimming across to the cliff we were swept fast through the dark, grabbing the rocks and clinging on, feeling the pull of the river.

Honey, compelled by some fascinating scent or other, kept swimming head first into a bush on the near bank; I heard a rustling crunch, and could barely make her out – like the moon, just a white blur behind the tangle of branches. As I pulled her out and pointed her towards the step, she turned and shot straight back in using a combination of super-doggy-paddle and a leaping dive. I retrieved her again, again she dived back. I persuaded her to get out, and she careered back into the bush from the top in a crash of splintering wood, snorting and snuffling.

The river was a couple of feet higher than usual. Drifts of leaves stroked us as we swam through brief flashes of copper. The sky cleared, stars appeared. The wispy white clouds began to reflect moonlight, and finally the moon rose above the trees; we swam in the shadow cast by the cliff, looking across the common to where hawthorns stood petrified like witches in the glow. A mist appeared like ectoplasm and wrapped itself around the distant trees.

BLACKPOOL SANDS
13 November
~

A beautiful November day; cool blue sky, a faint mist and an onshore hoolie blowing. Fine, ginger-coloured shingle and opaque, greeny-turquoise sea met in a foaming clatter of shore-break; the retreating waves left with a sound like summer rain.

We porpoised through the surf to the waves that rushed diagonally across the bay. They grew in stature as we swam out to sea, cresting through white horses and dropping into troughs. In the distance, spray splattered the reefs marking the edges of the bay. I felt I could swim forever out to sea, cradled by waves.

Turning back reluctantly, I aimed for the group on the shore and swam along the waves, rising then dropping precipitously. Finally, I raced for the shore between breaks, and avoided being slapped into the beach. It looked and smelled like summer.

TORQUAY
22 November
~

There's something about approaching the sea on a November evening, under wreaths of coloured lights. Low tide, cold concrete steps, chilled sand, water that feels warm as summer. We swam in the dark, a few stars twinkled above, and the lights reflected in the water. Floating on my back, my feet froze till I drew them back under the blanket of sea.

PLYMOUTH HOE
27 November

~

It's a beautiful morning and the sea sparkles; grey Naval ships are silhouetted on the horizon. We descend the Art Deco steps, worn into natural shapes by eighty years of storms and tides, and trip through the stones on the tiny beach. Joh's dad beats us in, then returns immediately to shore as though attached to a bungee. 'You need to stay in for twenty minutes to get the benefits!' I say. He gives me an old-fashioned look.

Joh, Pauline and I swim to the buoy marking the edge of the swimming area, then turn parallel to the rocky shore. If you venture too far out here you're liable to be sunk by a warship, mangled in the propellers of a cross-channel ferry, or surprised from underneath by a submarine.

After a while we float and enjoy the view: Smeaton's Tower and the big wheel on the shore; Drake's Island over towards the Tamar; and the Breakwater a couple of miles out in the Sound. Turning back, the current is surprisingly strong around the tiny promontory, and – swimming just a few meters further from shore than Pauline and Joh – I realise suddenly that I'm way behind them.

I look up at the sky; icy blue and bisected by a cloud the colour and shape of a flatfish skeleton.

PLYMOUTH HOE
30 November

~

Pauline and I looked over the railings on Plymouth Hoe into the maelstrom below. Wooo hooo!

Down the steps we went to the now invisible little beach, dodging the waves that surged over the walkway. Pauline is acclimatising for a Channel relay, so she sat shivering on the steps in her cossie and her new yellow 'Devon and Cornwall Wild Swimming' hat, hoping that the spray would serve as a gentle introduction to the fast-cooling sea. As I struggled with my wetsuit zip, I heard a shriek accompanied by a crash and clatter as Pauline vanished in a vast white cloud. I watched the step where she had been as the spray dispersed, but she was gone. I scanned the sea. After twenty seconds or so I spotted a flash of yellow about fifty yards away. Luckily, Pauline was still attached to it, so I plunged in and followed her out.

Waves the colour of pewter smacked my face and I bounced in all directions as I tried to swim a course to the buoy that appeared between the lumps in a series of increasingly crazy angles. Pauline and I laughed and pinged around in the brine, watching the spray flying and smelling the scent of stormy sea. On the horizon, near the breakwater, two warships sheltered. The brightness of the horizon narrowed to a slash as a bank of swirling cloud loomed overhead, reflecting the temperament of the sea.

We swam from buoy to buoy, often exceeding the 4 knots speed limit with a little help from Neptune. Finally, having reached maximum exhilaration, we set off back in and were dumped inelegantly on the shore.

Stripping off, Pauline shed a beach load of shingly sand from her swimsuit.

LONDON BRIDGE
3 December

~

Secreted just around the corner from Torquay Harbour is a tiny beach from where you can swim around jaunty rock islets to London Bridge, a limestone arch jutting from a small headland. It's chilly in the December sea, and we laugh at Stephanie bobbing in her wetsuit while holding her hands out of the water to keep them warm.

We're floating in deep turquoise, and pale slabs of tumbled cliff litter the seabed. The bridge leans tipsily against the headland, its arch a precarious conglomeration of vertical slabs, gravel and earth.

We are sucked through, and I lie on my back beneath the jagged silhouette as the sea slaps against the rocks.

Further on, Sophie has found a cave. We swim towards it, a tall, dark slit rising from petrol blue sea in the corner where the headland meets the cliff. Generations of barnacles crowd the limestone forming a pock-marked skin of bumps and promontories, acned by a splattering of white and yellow whelks. Water and weed run off as the waves ebb, and the sound echoes and intensifies as we near the entrance to the cave.

Jonathan, Queenie and I follow Sophie in. Overhead there is darkness except for a crack of light far above, but we are suspended in luminous water that shooshes with the pulse of the ocean. We whoop and cackle when a big wave pushes us up and up towards the cave roof and scream as we drop back down.

There are supposed to be conger eels here in the womb of the cliffs, and we await the snap of giant fishy jaws from beneath.

21

I have a sudden shock as I bob under and see an eel-like strand of weed curling around our legs.

CHARLESTOWN
4 December
~

To get to the sea at Charlestown, you pass the Museum of Shipwrecks and a couple of tall ships in the dock. Cold, grey sea and splatting rain marked our arrival and we set off on a proper swim, by which I mean full throttle and no exploring. One of the Plymouth contingent was so fast she left a wake, and as Hugo said, 'kept going back and forth between groups like a Labrador.' It was calmer than it's been for a while, so swimming was easy. We headed from point to point and stopped occasionally to regroup, watching people watching us from the harbour wall and the nearby beaches. A group of cormorants sat on a rock; I was tempted to join them.

Eventually, we turned back. I got into the zone and kept going through my tiredness, swimming alongside Kirsty. We realised we'd been pushed too far by the current and had to swim back towards the beach through a miasma of poo.

I finally got my feet down close to the steep, shingle beach and staggered to the shore. A wave around four inches high knocked me sideways before my blood-pressure had adjusted. I was completely unable to stand, and washed around in the wavelets, spreadeagled and wrecked on this shore like so many ships before me.

We changed in the wind tunnel at the top of the beach. I warmed up by helping a puffing Hugo out of his new wetsuit, which is formed from several overlapping layers like a corn cob.

DOUBLE DART
10 December

~

It's December, the air temperature is 7 degrees, and the water half a degree less. Honey and I stride through the woods, dead leaves squidging underfoot like soggy cornflakes. We stop opposite Wellsfoot Island.

In the summer, I dislike swimming here as Holne cliff exerts then a looming oppression over the otherwise lovely pool beneath. Today it's inviting: blue-black water glinting in the blue-grey light; the surrounding space expanded by the view through denuded winter trees; the soughing of the rapids like a lullaby. The tiny red sandy beach on the island is partly hidden by a drift of dark twigs a couple of feet deep. Behind is moss and desiccated bracken the colour of a fox's pelt.

I change into my wetsuit and Honey swims over to the Island, where she rootles around and finds an old shoe which provides entertainment for the duration of my swim. I walk carefully over the rocky bed to the deeper water and feel the change from my last (11 degrees) swim here. I dive forwards and the river slashes me like a blade. In her winter guise she has lost her silky, peat-scented enchantment and become a steel-hard witch with the taste and texture of bootleg vodka. My hands, face and neck burn with cold and I feel my blood freezing. A flock of kayakers zip by; one of them shouts "People think we're mad!"

I swim hard through the current to the bank, then lie on my back watching the ice-blue sky till the cold is too much. As I change, tendrils of mist emanate from my skin. We start to walk back and I realise the scalding heat I feel is actually the frost radiating from my bones.

PLYMOUTH HOE
11 December
~

I thought it would be simple to get into the stormy Sound at low tide, but the rocky shore scuppered our easy entry and my bare feet protested at the battering they took. The water temperature had dropped to 10.9 degrees since our swim last week – a small but noticeable difference.

Murky, slaty-green sea slapped our faces; our bodies rocked randomly in the ragged waves. Our view of the Hoe was misted by spray. We swam around the point, striking out a little way to avoid being dashed onto rocks. After 45 minutes I was chilled to the core.

I stood on the wet concrete under the arches and stripped while the wind stole the last of the warmth from my body. My feet had no feeling and my hands fumbled with my clothes.

Clutching my hot cappuccino later, I was tempted to pour it into my boots.

BURGH ISLAND
24 December
~

There was a bully of a breeze blowing as I changed into my wetsuit for our Christmas Eve swim. It's a wild and beautiful spot, juxtaposed with the identikit bungalows littering the cliff at Bigbury-on-Sea, and the famous Art Deco Burgh Island Hotel. People who live around here all wear navy blue Baker Boy hats and clothes decorated with anchors, but I suspect that most of them don't go into the sea.

White horses in abundance and a murky, slaty-blue sea beckoned.

Several Santas, a few silly hats and some slightly more sensible swimmers skipped into the festive fizz. Prize for the funkiest outfit went to Jackie, who managed to look glamorous with blue skin in a giant white hair pom-pom and a Santa mini-dress. JJ started in a Santa suit, then realised it wasn't possible to swim round in it so stripped to reveal a wetsuit. Rudolph the red-nosed reindeer had hitched a lift on my head, but he sadly became waterlogged and floated off towards the shore on his own. Hopefully he won't be too cold to fly later on.

The dippers bobbed and swam around for a while and then went off for hot drinks, while eight of us decided to swim round the island. Jo, Sophie and I floated off to look at the famous gully which we were hoping to navigate. The sea was huge on the windward side of the island though, and the gap was largely invisible thanks to churning froth and spume.

We headed back out from the rocks. I felt myself being flung around by the waves, many of which were pointed like snow-capped mountains. A couple broke over me, some directly into my mouth. Occasionally a cold wall of sea walloped me in the head so hard that I was knocked backwards, my ears brimful and the sound of the ocean fading to an echo. When I rolled to breathe I had to look before inhaling. The feeling is both exhilarating and scary; you swim along, and suddenly you're flung one way, then another, then you stop dead, engulfed. You're picked up and lifted skywards before plummeting into the trough of a wave.

I glimpsed the others around forty yards away and swam towards them. Saw Sophie illuminated briefly by a flash of sunlight against the dark cliffs, swimming along the crest of a huge wave with her blue fins waving, a crazy mermaid. The wave smashed into the rocks, she vanished behind the next swell and I didn't see her again.

On the seaward side of the island, the rollers came at us from behind and we had a turbo-charged surf towards the hotel. The sun broke through again and I felt the warmth on my chilled face. Bubbles made by my stroke mingled with the foam to turn silver in the sea.

We tried to reach the beach through the rock reef, but it was too rough, so we headed back out and round the edge. Talking to Kirsty I was slurring my words and realised my mouth was frozen. We looked around but still couldn't see Sophie. Then, after a few minutes, she reappeared in the shallows with JJ in tow, having lured him to Mermaid's Pool, a serene oasis beside the hotel.

SPITCHWICK
25 December
~

A Saturnalia swim. The river is up, but not too angry today, and the coppery water is 8 degrees. I decide to go without my wetsuit, and wear instead my wet rash vest from yesterday's swim, a pair of patchwork hippie shorts, and wetsuit boots, plus my floral hat. The five of us plunge straight in: Joh, Jackie, Lesley, Honey and me.

Icy water squeezes my chest and sends chills like needles up my neck. We're all shrieking and screaming, and the shrill sounds cut through my body. Within a minute or so, I am burning up and numb. I make a conscious effort to unclench my shoulders and swim upstream on the slow side in staccato breaststroke. Jackie, as usual, is grinning broadly and swimming serenely as though the water were tropical. Lesley passes me in front crawl which splatters the surface with tiny balls of water that roll around for a few seconds before vanishing back into the river. Honey crashes festively into a holly bush on the bank.

After ten minutes we leap out and change, skin as red as holly berries. We toast Saturnalia and midwinter with gluhwein, gingerbread, mince pies and a Bonio.

SHARRAH
27 December
~

Sharrah Pool on the Double Dart. A calm, warmish winter's day. JJ and Stephanie arrived from their 'Wildathlon' which involved a cycle ride from Ashburton, a run to Sharrah, a swim, and then back. Honey ran nuttily after squirrels, while I speed-walked to join in with the dip.

The water was around 8 degrees. 'This is really quite warm,' I said, as I swam out from the rocks, still glowing from my 30-minute pant through the winter woods. JJ had been in for a couple of minutes by then, and some unusual strangled sounds were still audible above the surge of the river where he swam in head-up front crawl. He had the look of Conan the Barbarian on a dangerous mission. A school of kayaks overtook him as he tried to look even more cool (not difficult in this temperature) by floating casually on his back.

I began to breaststroke upstream, quickly dipping my salty, sweaty face in the lovely, bog-brown water. Suddenly, my body realised how cold it was as the river stole the last of the heat from my muscles. I looked towards the falls, hoping that the sight of such beauty would stun the pain. Stephanie stood on the rock up to her knees, and with encouragement from JJ dunked in, pulling the kind of face you normally only see on a woman in the final stages of labour. She shot back out like a champagne cork, to be quickly joined by me. Refreshing. Yes. Very.

2012

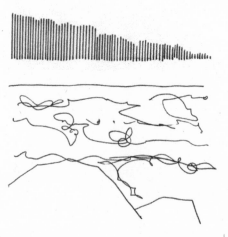

FINGLE BRIDGE
13 January
~

Two weeks of non-swimming with a virus meant I was ready for a refreshing dip with Dan in the Teign at Fingle Bridge. Honey and I arrived and walked to the bridge; a scene of muted winter-woodland colours livened by splashes of fox-coloured beech leaves. The river here is murkier than the Dart – the colour (and temperature) of brass monkeys.

We walked up through the gorge, nippy air and diaphanous mist curling from the river's surface. Sounds came and went: the crash of Honey hurtling after squirrels; the odd drift of birdsong, watery plinks and tinkles; a crescendo of white noise from the salmon leaps below Castle Drogo. We had hoped to dip here in the crazy cold jacuzzi, but the surge of angry water looked wilder than our bodies could withstand.

I wore my surfing wetsuit and boots. Standing thigh-deep in the pool, I felt the icy fingers of 6-degree water scratch at my calves. My hands burned with cold, my head felt as though it was in a vice and my vision was blurred by mist emanating from the water. I managed to swim for around a minute before leaping out.

Dan bravely floated up and down wearing only his budgie-smugglers, though I suspect his budgies were hiding higher up. He leapt out with skin glowing brighter than the logs in the pub wood-burner where we warmed up afterwards.

LONDON BRIDGE

14 January

~

A chilly-willy winter day with a brisk south-easterly tousling the white-capped swell. It's almost low tide, and the tiny beach at Peaked Tor Cove is rocky and draped with glistening seaweeds. The raw slap of sea soon becomes tolerable and then exhilarating, and I strike out round the rocks through opaque, pale turquoise water, buffeted and bounced by the chop. Waves fling spray into the air around the arch, and water sluices through from behind.

We head for the sea cave and watch for a while, but it's too dangerous. Rollers surge in to the narrow inlet and – split by the submerged rocks – churn around inside, making escape difficult. The sea billows increase as we approach the back of the arch to see whether that might be passable. JJ cannot be dissuaded, and he sets off with Hugo and me watching carefully to see whether he makes it. We catch an occasional flash of his blue hat amid the maelstrom, then swim round to find he's reappeared in a rather more dishevelled state than when he entered. Startled eyes and a wonky, frozen mouth soon remodel into a grin. He says he got stuck in a little pool left by the retreating waves for a bit, but still offers to go back with me. I'm tempted but feel cold now, so I decline.

It's easier returning with the wind and waves. From time to time the sun partially breaks through leaden clouds and shoots rays of light which glimmer off the surface, like an illustration in a children's Bible. As I roll to breathe I see a low-flying cormorant, neck extended, a couple of feet away. I arrive at the beach and manage to affect a staggering, shivering exit onto the pebbles. The contrast in how I feel by comparison to yesterday is dramatic. The sea is warmer than the river, but it's still cold. The character of water changes with the temperature: chilled river water is metallic and hard-edged; cold sea water, while abrasively salty, is somehow softer, bouncier and, well, more cuddly.

WEMBURY

21 January

~

An onshore wind and a rising tide on a mostly overcast day. The blue-grey light flattens the Mewstone into a predatory shark's fin on the horizon, and a stand-up paddle boarder seems to walk on water like Jesus. Surfers ride the breakers towards the reef below the Old Mill. The cloud breaks briefly over the sea leaving a silver puddle shimmering like a net full of mackerel in the distance.

We leap through the surf wooo-hoooing; every so often we wimp out in the teeth of a monster wave and dive under, chilly water surging down through the necks of our suits. I hear white noise, and the roar of the big rollers reach a crescendo as they break. Ducking under, I am surrounded by the same sounds muffled through my swim hat, mingled with bubbles as I exhale. The water is a dull greeny-turquoise, murky with smashed fragments of green-brown seaweed.

We swim for around forty minutes, buffeted by the crazy sea, rising then crashing back into troughs, lips shrivelled by brine. I can feel the wind ripping the warmth from my head. The Mewstone mermaid is calling us, but we're cold and it's way too rough for even JJ and his fins to obey. We'll save that swim for the spring.

ANSTEY'S COVE

21 January

~

I drive across the moors through tipping rain to meet Dangerous

Malcolm (so named as the only person ever to swim to Thatcher Rock and live to tell the tale) for an aquatic exploration of Anstey's Cove in Torquay. The rain has pretty much stopped, and I'm stunned by the scene out over the cove which resembles a 1970s album cover, all fantasy rocks and glassy water, framed by skeletal trees.

It's low tide and, as we begin to swim, I realise it's been weeks since I've seen such a calm, pale sea, which merges with the rippled, dove-grey sky in a vision of utter tranquility. We head for the witch's hat, near which is a small doorway in the cliff. The water here is a deep azure, darkening as we near the cave. I feel big raindrops plopping onto my head. Stumbling over a submerged rock in the narrow fissure, I follow Malcolm into a magical private world. Illuminated by a skylight some yards above is a mini-amphitheatre, and at the far end a tiny, shingle beach where the sea shushes in and out. The limestone has been rounded and smoothed by the waves. At high tide, the cave must be completely submerged.

On the other side of the point is an even tinier slit, which I enter warily. There's barely any headroom and even on such a calm day there's a yard or so of rise and fall from the funnelling effect of the narrow opening. Suddenly, Malcolm shoots past me on a surge, and I watch his head rising into the roof and his neck buckling as the sea engulfs him. For a couple of seconds, I wonder where he is; then there's a sucking noise as the sea retreats and he reappears cackling, pretty much where I last saw him. He continues deeper into the cave, and I examine the Dead Men's Fingers clinging to the rock, like the remains of a previous Dangerous Malcolm.

We swim on to a large gap in the cliff shaped like a theatre stage. I hear cooing and see two doves rather incongruously perched inside. The smell of bird shit pervades. Here the sea is a luminous aquamarine and the slabs of damp, barnacled rock are splattered with clashing rust-red sea-life which causes the colours to sing like a Matisse painting. I film underwater and don't notice I'm being picked up by a surge until I crash backwards into a protruding cheese-grater of a stone. As I right myself and rub my elbow, Malcolm is ripped almost out of the cave through a channel to the side of the rock by what looks like a river rapid. He swims back in, giggling.

As we exit, I swim face down. There is sand as pale as a bald pate in winter, tufted with clumps of seaweed like a bad hair-transplant. I roll onto my back and see that the tops of the cliff are similarly adorned with fine-twigged bushes. I already know this is a world bursting with life, and it's easy to imagine that we're exploring the body of a fairy tale monster.

The cold gets us in the end, and we decide it's sensible to return now, so we swim back in front crawl. I struggle to stay upright on the rocky beach and lean forwards with my hands on my knees. I glance back at the surreal world we've just left; it seems like a dream.

BURGH ISLAND
28 January

~

A sunny, calm afternoon for a swim and beach party to celebrate the birthdays of Stephanie and Kari. Jonathan inflated red heart balloons with helium and attached them to each swimmer; my heart gathered sea-drops and hovered just above the surface as I swam.

We found the entrance to Death Valley, the fearsome gully

between the island and the high part of the reef; today in the calm low tide only a ghostly presence was manifest. As the tide swooshed in and out, submerged seaweeds flowed one way then the other like mermaid hair. Pale pink rocks sang through pale blue water.

Cormorants and oystercatchers flew towards land, the latter filling the air with their squeaky-toy calls. Gulls settled down to roost as the sun dropped lower. The cool shades of blue and grey where sea met sky were infused with a pinky-peach layer like strawberry jelly in a trifle. The surface of the water assumed the texture and colour of mercury in the metallic light.

I'd have loved to dawdle, but it was way too cold, so I swam the back of the island in front crawl and worked my way through the rocky maze below the hotel, before running across the sand-bar to our spot below the Pilchard Inn.

I managed to change despite the coarse shivering that indicates mild hypothermia. Then we shared snacks, home-made cakes, mulled cider and Prosecco and sang Happy Birthday as the sun set. A perfect afternoon.

SHARRAH
4 February
~

High on Dartmoor, the Double Dart slows briefly between two sets of rapids to form Sharrah Pool. There are plenty of breathtakingly beautiful places on this stretch of river, but Sharrah is special. It's enchanting, entrancing, and it never fails to throw buckets of Dartmoor pixie-dust at anyone who sees it.

Today there is a sprinkling of snow and it's still falling as we arrive in the glade by the pool. The temperature hasn't gone above freezing for days; it's 3 degrees in the river. The water is much paler than usual and has lost its deep coppery gleam and black depths. By the rapids there's a gelid, greeny tint that I've never seen here before.

Wearing wetsuits, boots, gloves and hats, we slide into the river and swim up the eddy towards the top falls. Ice creeps through the neck of my suit. I dip my face under and taste pure chill; my lips freeze almost immediately. We reach the rapid and throw ourselves off the rock. It's like jumping into a beautiful cocktail made with crème de menthe and the most effervescent volcanic water. The bubbles burst fast on the surface in a shower of sparks like fireworks, and I can hear the fizz above the roar of the waterfall. Then I shoot along as though in the tail of a comet.

Snowflakes drift past. Icicles coat the rocks at the falls, and it's hard to tell them from the gushing spumes of water. The boulders in the glade are iced with snow. Honey jumps between them, following us upstream.

My fingers slowly freeze from the tips down, and after fifteen minutes or so I'm forced to leave this magical water world. We change, eat shortbread and drink hot chocolate. We dip our fingers in warm water from a flask. Mine are blue and the intense pain whirls me back to my childhood of wet wool socks in wellingtons and winter chilblains.

MAIDENCOMBE
10 February

~

South-easterlies scuppered our plans to explore along the coast at low tide today, with a hefty swell and a force 4 to 5 wind.

The sea churned with dark red sand and transmogrified into that tastefully dull taupe colour currently found on so many interior walls. The shallows were a chunky winter soup of seaweeds and flotsam.

Swimming out to sea, I plunged head first through heavy breakers. As I swam, wave turrets hit me from all angles and I began to swallow water. Looking round, I realised we'd been carried alongshore and were close to the rocks. Spray splattered the air. I struck out seawards and then back along towards the beach, pushed and pulled by the surging water. Dangerous Malcolm meanwhile appeared on the rocks and walked back around to the beach before returning to the sea; he told me later he'd been unable to swim away against the force of the waves and had to land instead.

Back in the relatively calm area off the beach, I floated around and played in the surf, watched by sandstone cliffs the colour of dried blood.

WEMBURY
11 February
~

A chilly, still, slightly overcast afternoon and a very low tide. The scent of seaweed and fish. A dog charges around, playing with a long-dead rabbit. The peach-coloured light brings out the steely blue-greys of the sea, and the sun forces her way through intermittently with wondrous effects. Beams of light splay around the Mewstone, and the horizon is lit briefly by a line like burning phosphorous.

The water is cold, around 7.5 degrees, and my face freezes painfully. Several people are seriously underdressed for the occasion, and even Pauline grimaces for several seconds before launching into a solo synchronised swimming routine. Joh, on the other hand, appears to be entering the water wearing a puffa jacket. Ninja Elf is recognisable only by her squeals, muffled through the balaclava.

We swim out, then return fairly quickly with cold hands and numb toes. A fast change and we refuel with two types of cake. As we leave, we're enveloped by the distant sounds of kids laughing and the slap of Honey's feet as she gallops along the wet sand.

ODDICOMBE
20 February
~

A steep walk down the lane past Babbacombe Cliff Railway, with glimpses of glassy sea through naked trees. Hunks of sandstone cliff from a recent landslide litter the far end of the beach with a monumental jumble studded with grey pebbles and the remains of a hideously expensive garden.

We swim around the cliffs through nippy, chalky-blue water, and encounter a cave almost immediately. Here the limestone cliffs seem stained and pitted by the sea, but a closer inspection reveals a three-dimensional mosaic of sea life: barnacles; a variety of tiny anemone bodies in shades of brown; bilious algae; a burnt-orange, gelatinous splat of a creature; Dead Men's Fingers in white.

We enter the cave which extends far above us. Waves surge up the narrowing fissure and carry us in before sucking us back, cradled by the sea. Sophie and Susie climb a rock and discover a pool like an oyster in a dark, shell-shaped cavern. They sit on the ledge to one side, which overlooks the rest of the cave.

Matt floats in the pool, and the flash from my camera illuminates this magical place, transforming it.

We swim on over seaweeds like flowers against a sea-blue sky, rocks splodged with pink and maroon algae, and constellations of starfish in orange and cream. I float into a nook that reeks of fish. Juvenile mussels line the rock, and as the swell recedes, rivulets of water run then drip down with a sound like spring rain.

WEMBURY
25 February
~

Today we met at Wembury again – it's become the regular, winter sea-swim for some of us. Spring is in the air and the sun has real warmth, burning through the mist by lunchtime. We swim out hard towards the Mewstone, visible in three dimensions in the bright sunshine but never seeming to get any closer. This will be our big planned swim for when the sea warms. We cut back towards the Yealm side, and feel the power of the reef reeling us in. It's easy to imagine ships coming to grief here as the waves build, break and suck with the funnelling effect of the submerged rocks.

Later, we change and play ball with Honey and Mary, a bull terrier. There is a dog hater on the beach, identifiable by her chilling laser-stares at any canines and their humans who dare to venture within half a mile. Mary spots her at once, shoots over with her comical gambolling canter, and sticks her head into Mrs Dog Hater's takeaway box – which quite possibly contains minced dog burgers.

We wander along the coast path to Heybrook Bay, which allows us a closer look at the Mewstone from Wembury Point – a mere half a kilometre from here, but with a strong current through the narrows.

The fields behind the path are dotted with plump rabbits and oystercatchers, mingling as though at a cocktail party.

SHARRAH
28 February
~

Sharrah Pool, low water for winter, and an incredible 9 degrees today. The spooky greens and blues have pretty much gone now it's warmed up, although there is a hint of urine mixed with loo-blue about the rapids. Honey and I swim across the centre of the pool and I push her soggy bum up onto the rocks so she can go exploring. I glide up the central eddy and back down through the fizz, then decide to put in some effort and hit the rapids against the current.

I reach and slide in crawl as far as the big rock. Suddenly water surges over my head and arm, I sink lower and almost inhale river rather than air. I realise I'm about to collide with the ledge on the far bank. I try again, eyeballs chilled as I'm not wearing goggles, and again hit the weird combination of oppositional force and lack of buoyancy.

I rest on the rock, and Honey appears on the far side of the falls. She goes in, and plummets beneath the surface, beginning to panic as her heavy coat combines with the foaming rapids to pull her down. I jump in and support her beneath the ribs, and we descend the river together. She hauls herself out, a matt of soggy ringlets, and tries to dry her ears by rubbing her nose sideways along the ground.

41

EXMOUTH
9 March
~

It's a good idea for a wild swimmer to master the necromancy of wind, tide, currents and waves, and so it was that my friend Steph the Ninja Elf and I went to Exmouth to do the RLSS Beach Lifeguard Qualification.

The first hint that this might not be as simple as running up and down in slo-mo with artfully tousled hair and a rescue tube came when Steph noticed that the run and swim times for different age-groups in our Beach Lifeguard Manual stopped at age 39.

The second came in the pool when Bongo, our 23-year-old course mate, swam 400m in around thirty-two seconds and then told us how much faster he'd been as a youth, when he would finish the swim before he'd started.

The third involved getting to grips with the rescue tubes, by which time we were too tired to even attempt to look good, and too out of breath to hum the Baywatch theme tune again. I had thought 'porpoising' was simply forging head-first, arms over head through a wave. Wrong! Porpoising is the Beach Lifeguard technique for entering the sea with a rescue tube and involves a five-mile run through dry sand, sprinting to knee-depth with the loop at the end of the eight-foot strap over your head and one shoulder, throwing the tube out and to one side, diving gracefully into the sea and hitting the sand, grabbing the sand so as not to be wiped out by a wave, resisting hyperventilating with cold-shock, pushing off the sand with one leg while trying to disentangle the rescue tube strap from your other leg while your neck is hyper-extended, after which you briefly appear – like a porpoise – above the waves before plunging back in and repeating the manoeuvre once or twice more because it's 'faster' than swimming.

You then swim flat out while keeping your head up, supposedly so the casualty doesn't vanish while you're not looking, but actually because the strap is still wrapped round your neck and one leg. You then throw the tube at them without knocking them out with the metal clip, persuade them to turn around so they won't attack you, clip the tube around them while they scream, punch you, rip out a hunk of hair, and pull you under with the strap because you've forgotten to slip it over your head and it's still wrapped around one leg.

After this, you're expected to tow the casualty – formerly your friend but whom you are now starting to dislike intensely – back to the beach while they laugh openly at your gasping attempt at swimming with 'urgency'. You hug them supportively and act looking at them in a caring way while you carry them ashore, resisting the urge to knee them in the back and stamp on their head.

Finally, if you're still alive, you have to carry a ten-foot Malibu board at speed through a howling crosswind down a mined RNLI slipway to the sea. You then execute a warp factor, two-armed paddle to deep water, flip the board over next to the casualty while inhaling a wave, paddle sideways while coughing up seawater on the upside-down board to try to catch the casualty who's being swept away at 5 knots by the estuarine current while the wind and waves push you in the opposite direction, before inhaling sufficient air to turn the casualty over and give five rescue breaths.

After this the casualty is miraculously supposed to be lying on the board in the right place to allow you to hop onto the back without sinking or pushing the nose under. Self, casualty and board should all now be facing the shore, ready for you to paddle self and casualty back to the beach with your face buried in their bum.

43

Throughout the entire rescue you have, of course, been keeping one eye on the beach where Andy the Instructor is rapidly flapping his arms, one of which is holding a shark-warning flag while the other is simultaneously spelling out in Lifeguard Sign Language a critique of your efforts so far, the speed and direction of the current, warnings of approaching dumping waves, a reprimand for not knowing how to tie a head-bandage, a request for you to sign back three types of rip current, and a record of which bits of your kit passing dogs have just pissed on.

To our utter amazement, we both passed, although it was made quite clear that we're too slow to get actual Beach Lifeguard jobs on beaches longer than twelve feet or with a tidal range of more than two inches. Nonetheless, a fantastic week during which we learned a huge amount.

THATCHER ROCK
18 March

~

Thatcher Rock: an innocuous-looking, volcano-shaped island speckled with seabirds and bright green vegetation, a couple of hundred metres off Hope's Nose. Now this is where things get scary: to get to the Rock, you have to cross the little channel attractively named The Gut. The bit you swim from forms part of a promontory on the edge of a large bay; the combination of narrow channel and point means fast tidal currents. The only person we know who has achieved this, and who was named for this very feat of derring-do, is Dangerous Malcolm. He and Sophie had now hatched a plot to stage a group assault.

When we arrived just before high tide, the sea was the colour of a storm cloud. A shower quickly passed, and we made our way to the cliff's edge, from where we scrambled down the narrow, slippery track to the cliff fall near the beach. Finn, Guardian of the Keys, had brought a yellow umbrella and used that to fly down like Mary Poppins. Ninja Elf had met a German family and invited them – they bravely followed us over the edge for their first Devon Wild Swim, despite their obvious misgivings.

In order to stake a claim to the Rock, JJ had brought a Jordanian flag, and Jackie had made a Devon Wild Swimmers flag in turquoise and red, which she gave to Dangerous Malcolm. There was some hilarious discussion about where to put the poles. Dangerous Malcolm has recently been cultivating a rather luscious and spiky explorer-type, perma-frosted beard. With his stocky frame and rubber swimming hat atop his neoprene hood, side flaps flipped casually up, he resembled the love-child of Scott of the Antarctic and Amelia Earheart. JJ, in an attempt to float his legs for his upcoming Channel swim, has allegedly gained a kilo by eating lots of cakes.

We plunged into gin-clear sea as the sun appeared, following Sophie and her coterie over fallen rocks piled up like sugar cubes. For the first time in months my face didn't freeze. I swam easily and arrived at the Rock in what seemed like a couple of minutes; I stopped and trod water, then realised I was heading away from the little gaggle hanging on to the rock at about 2 knots. Bearing in mind we swam at slack tide, this was pretty impressive. The cries of gulls and the stench of fish surrounded us. I swam hard to the up-current side of the island, and spent a while floating and watching the shags, perched and silhouetted along the top of the Rock like gangs of 1950s bikers with their slick quiffs.

Around the back were more shags, a couple of birds I didn't recognise and some cormorants. The sea here is deep, bluey, and clouded by semi-dissolved guano. As JJ and I rounded the corner to the sheltered side of the island, Dangerous Malcolm and flag

45

executed a perfect landing. JJ went to help with its erection while I took photos from the sea, buffeted by an increasing swell.

Finally, we set off back across The Gut, where the current appeared to have slackened slightly more. I made a couple of adjustments and got back fairly swiftly. In the shallows were more sugar-cube rocks covered in lettuce-green algae, and several types of delicate weed, one in bright orange. We clambered back up the cliff, happy and thrilled to have been involved in such a magical swim, and to have made it back without being swept away up the coast – a definite possibility on a spring tide.

BLACK ROCK
20 March

~

Honey and I pootled over to the River Lyd this afternoon for a revivifying skinny-dip in Witch's Pool.

As we wandered upstream through the valley, Honey disturbed a young vixen who shot out under her nose from a gorse thicket and zig-zagged off up Widgery Tor, her brush going like a metronome to balance her flight. Honey continued to sniff excitedly in the thicket, having missed the entire escape. We then saw an elderly man who reacted in much the same way as the vixen had and shot off up the tor perpendicular to the track in order to avoid us.

We scrambled down the steep valley side and I stripped quickly, sliding into the chilly pool from a granite boulder. I ducked under the clear brown water, and as I popped back up and floated through the familiar ache of cold skin, a skylark sang overhead echoing the tumbling course of the little river. Honey played in the shallows and the elderly man reappeared around a hundred yards away, freezing in a cartoon pose as he caught sight of me, before hurrying off back downstream. I dried by jigging on the grass to the clacking whistle of a wheatear, although I couldn't see it.

I thought – as I always do when we come here – of the young soldier whose verse, written during a leave shortly before his death, is attached to Black Rock above a wooden bench:

Are we not like this moorland stream,
Springing none knows where from,
Tinkling, bubbling, flashing a gleam,
Back at the sun 'ere long,
Gloomy and dull under a cloud,
Then rushing onwards again,
Dashing at rocks with anger loud,
Roaring and foaming in vain,
Wandering thus for many a mile,
Twisting and turning away for a while,
Then of a sudden 'tis over the fall,
And the dark still pool is the end of all.
Is it? I thought as I turned away,
And I turned away to the silent moor.
'Is it?' I said and my heart said 'Nay',
As I gazed at the cross on Widgery Tor.

   – *Captain Nigel Duncan Ratcliffe Hunter, of Lydford,*
     killed in 1918, aged 23

DOUBLEWATERS
27 March

~

It's a sparkling, warm day and Honey and I decide to wander down to Doublewaters for a dip. The trees are still naked and look startled to be illuminated by such bright beams of sunlight, like wild swimmers caught skinny-dipping.

There's a slight haze and the wind swirls, carrying the bleats of newborn lambs, as we leave the open moor and enter the woods. We walk down the track through the precipitous valley and the tinkling sound of the Walkham river drifts to meet us. We arrive at the granite outcrop that marks the confluence of the two valleys and their rivers. The pool where we swim is on the Tavy side and looks enticing, slightly opaque and green-tinted, framed by bare trees and barred shadows.

I walk straight in over slippery rocks and go under, swimming up against the current. The water is still pretty chilly, and I get ice-cream cheeks today, but the warm air makes all the difference. The smell of baking leaf mould reminds me of summer. Floating on my back I hear quacking but can't see the ducks. A fish jumps with a plop. Honey is growling and digging her ball out of the shallows with her arse in the air. The sky is so blue against the silvery bark, lichen and ferns that it seems tangible; I feel I can float up into it.

THE LYD
30 March

~

Another stunning spring day, and I was foiled in my plans to do a food shop thanks to the pathetic petrol-queueing mayhem that gridlocked Tavistock. So off we went for a long walk and a swim instead – who needs food?

I love the moors on days like these: the hazy, dreamlike view of Brat Tor and Widgery Cross; the smell of sheep-wee; the bleats of the ewes just loosed back out to lamb; the intermittent early skylark songs, occasional bumblebees on gorse flowers.

I slid in on the shadowy side at Witch's Pool and swam into the light to warm, golden water. Rambling downstream, dipping in each of the tiny pools, pushed under by waterfalls and sinking through crystal bubbles, I drifted into daydreams.

SOAR MILL COVE
8 April
~

A gaggle of us ambled along the coast path from the cliff at Bolberry Down to Soar Mill Cove on a sunny, blowy day. En route, we found ourselves level with a hovering kestrel, which looked like a flying heart with its curved wings.

It felt like a summer's day on the beach with the sun, the blue sky and the sand pitted from the passing of many feet. We hung around in swimwear, although it was somewhat nippy in the breeze, and gaped at Jackie who, having swum in all weathers throughout the winter in a swimsuit, had decided to wear rubber 'to keep the heat out'. JJ changed into his new floating shorts, which contained Brazilian secret padded Envy Pants, increasing the size of his arse from two garden peas to a couple of apricots.

I ran into the sea, which was warmer than the puddles on the beach, and bobbed around for a bit. Most of the others set off to circumnavigate the Ham Stone, which looked wonderful. As I'm injured I stayed close to shore and then had to rescue Honey, who'd lost sight of me and run off along past the caves in a panic.

It was low tide on a spring, so we were able to explore the caves on foot. One cave went back some distance, but it was too dark inside to see much. There was a faint scent of city car park about it. It looks as though it would be easily swimmable, even on a high spring tide in decent conditions.

On the way back up, we saw our kestrel again and watched as she floated on the updrafts like a swimmer in a bouncy sea.

HORSESHOE FALLS
9 April
~

Queenie, Honey and I amble along through the rain and squelchy earth to Salter's Pool on the Double Dart. The water is chilly and lovely with its fresh, peaty taste and we quickly become warm as we swim. It's not quite deep enough to shoot properly over the shallow bit, but I manage to get a decent swoosh in the middle before grounding on a rock. I worry about Queenie, who is acclimatising for a Channel swim and wearing only a swimsuit. Being Queenie, she goes for it and laughs through the pain, leaving a smear of blood over the rocks.

We arrive at Horseshoe Falls and slide over into the jacuzzi. I love the feeling of sinking through the bubbles, which soften even cold water so it resembles a feather bed. We bob around, sink, and swim up and down enjoying the sensation. Honey likes to wander around on the ledge above Horseshoe but misjudges it today and slips over the edge into the falls, sinking. Queenie pulls her up and she climbs back, with the broken tennis ball still in her mouth.

We swim back up against the current and scramble over the shallows with difficulty. Even though the water is low, there's still some force and the rocks appear to be made from ice. A couple of mallards fly away upstream.

As we swim through the pool, the rain becomes heavier and the wind picks up. A big gust splats raindrops into the river and sends a shiver across the surface which runs right through my body. Honey goes loopy-doodle following a scent. We change into damp clothes and drip our way back to the bridge.

MAIDENCOMBE
9 April
~

Today we meet Sophie for another of her research swims. She's doing a talk about the history of wild swimming in Torquay.

The sky is bright blue, and the sea is that weird orangey-turquoise colour you find beneath the red beaches around here. We set off towards Watcombe and the Bell Arch. About half way there I start to feel my shoulder injury. The arch seems to call to me, a rust-red promontory topped by a grassy toupée, but I manage to resist and return sensibly to the beach in a slow, shoulder-friendly front crawl with maximum rotation and no pull. The others carry on and find their way barred by a large seal, who scares them out of the water then follows them back along to the beach, thrilling the kids on the rocks.

Standing halfway up the cliff, I watch for the others; they appear as small dots in rippled circles, their laughs coming and going on the breeze.

THE ERME
19 April
~

We trot up the path through Long Timber Woods the day after heavy downpours have left the moorland rivers in spates. Entering a large, deep pool I feel the chill of recent rain and swim in dark brown water before Maretta and I float and bump downstream over rocky shallows and falls.

Jackie joins us off and on, having never descended a river before. We slide over slabs into effervescent pools, popping up through the spray like ice cubes dropped into a G&T.

Many of the rocks are cushioned by thick moss, so we are spared a proper battering and it's unusually easy to stop or get clear of stronger currents and stoppers.

There's a six-foot drop off one side of a biggish waterfall into a mini-canyon between boulders, followed by a scarily turbulent sequence of falls.

I slide off the drop and tip up as I hit the deep water, emerging to see the edge of the more dangerous cascade approaching fast. I push back and am immediately submerged by the force of the water. I manage to escape, and Maretta follows me over. I wait and catch her hand to pull her clear.

Shivering, we leave the river and wend our way back up the path to the viaduct; the roar of the cascades fades into the roar of traffic climbing the hill.

WATERMOUTH BAY
28 April
~

We head up-county today, to the Atlantic below the wild cliffs of North Devon. The sea is pale turquoise through the trees, which are still stark in places but frilled with tiny new leaves. The scent of wild garlic wafts in the wind, white flowers explode above caterpillar-green leaves. We totter down precipitously wonky steps for a couple of hundred feet to the greyish-pink sand. The bay is shaped like a slice of melon, with a series of mini-coves bitten out, each containing its own small beach.

Andrew, Geoffrey and I swim across to the cave-pocked bluff. Here leans a wonky archway, the ledge below barely covered by water. Sea drives into the rocks, making the caves difficult to explore properly. It's not too cold, but I feel the wind-chill. I turn back to check Honey who runs along the beach and keeps swimming a little way out towards me before returning to shore.

The waves in the crescent bay, sheltered from the north-easterlies, are fairly smooth; but beyond the narrow sand neck – which joins the pointed islet like a polyp to the northern side of the bay – there is a foaming mass of crazy, four-foot breakers. Floating on my back, buffeted by the sea, I watch the wave-shapes of the cliffs, rumpled into fifty-foot points above me.

WEMBURY
11 May
~

High tide, big breakers, and off we go into the cloudy sea. It's chillier than usual after days of torrential rain. We swim a bit then float, spreadeagled and sparkling in the sun to warm our frozen cheeks. Wembury Church is a silhouette, moving further and further away. We realise we're quite far out, and swim back at an angle against the swell, which is pushing over towards the reef on the Yealm side.

I start to enjoy the breakers, shooting up and plummeting on the far side in a wild rollercoaster. Teri and Michelle are slightly further in. Suddenly there's a set of huge waves, around twelve feet high. Realising we're in the breaking zone, I sink to the bottom and pop up after the wave has passed, but the next one is on me. I dive through it and get rolled. We're out of our depth, and it's hard to overcome the buoyancy of the wetsuit.

I have to shove my camera down my front to concentrate fully on getting through the surf and try to cross parallel to the beach where the waves are less high. I'm braced and ready for the next onslaught, when the energy drops suddenly. Looking shoreward, I spot my friends among the foamy amoeba-shapes left by the waves. Teri has the expression of a stunned sea bass; she's been rolled and has lost her goggles, and her swimming hat is perched like a second head atop her hair. Michelle says she looks like Blackadder the First.

SPITCHWICK
16 May
~

Evening at Spitchwick. Warm sun, chill breeze, cold river. The surface is smooth like liquid brass, reflecting acid-green leafed trees. Occasionally the wind catches the water which wrinkles along its path. As I swim I hear birds, the ripples from my stroke, and plinks and plops as fish jump for midges near the bank. The sun is low and catches my eyes, sparkling from damp eyelashes. My skin burns with the cold.

STOKE BOAT YARD
17 May
~

Honey is usually happy on the beach, but today I turn to see her teetering on the edge of the rocks as the surf hits, from where she is washed in to join us. She swims in her speedboat stroke – head right up and forelegs pumping fast. She relaxes as she reaches us, and we accompany her back to the rocks where she somehow manages to land through the white water, which streams from her woolly coat.

We return for another buffeting; loose weed catches my face as I swim, like ghostly hands. I look back shoreward and see sparse bleached grasses, colourless cliffs and the dusty track. It reminds me of the setting for the final showdown in a Spaghetti Western, to the point that I can hear the spooky strains of Ennio Morricone in the wind.

There are sea anemones in the shallows. I hear crunching over the sound of the sea; Honey, having tired of eating seaweed, is snacking on molluscs, shells and all.

Later, Michelle realises we were swimming from Stoke Boat Yard, just along from the real Stoke Beach which is secreted around the corner behind a rocky headland.

BANTHAM
20 May
~

It's Kari's idea to float down the Avon Estuary to Bantham carrying decorated umbrellas – partly for the spectacle, and partly to see whether we can. We slip into cool water just after high tide on a warm evening. Most of us are carrying umbrellas adorned with everything from fish and ribbons to Christmas decorations.

The water is still and deep aquamarine, reflecting the few puffs of cloud. As we swim out from the shadow of the boathouse we are warmed by hazy sunlight. I carry my brolly in one hand and swim in sidestroke, swept along by the current like Mary

Poppins. I hear laughter as the others stream water in beads from their brollies like rain in the sunshine. Honey follows, chasing flotillas of seaweed and pouncing as the mood takes her. She trails gory green sea lettuce from her mouth.

As I reach the remaining small square of sand I float face down and watch empty shells and balls of seaweed scud by over the wrinkled sand. Wavelets hit from three directions pushing my body hither and thither and moving the submarine flotsam in sympathy. My view is intermittently clouded by little sandstorms where opposing waves hit. I roll over and watch a couple of umbrellas drift round the point to the beach.

BEL POOL
21 May

~

Glorious sunshine. The scent of bluebells. May trees exploding. A soft carpet of grasses, wood anemones, mosses and leftover autumn leaves. As we walk, I watch the sky glaring blue through illuminated young oak leaves. I briefly mistake a yellow-green brimstone butterfly for a magically animated leaf.

We arrive at Bel Pool, a beguiling potion of reflected sun, frog-green light, dappled amber water and sparkling rapids. I climb in over a tree skeleton, washed here over the winter. The rocks below the surface are slippery, and I reach out to grab one near the surface. It feels like a hairy thigh with its patchy moss pelt. It's the warmest water I've swum in this year, but still tastes fresh and lovely as I push upstream.

I hear a tinkling like raindrops and feel the chill emanating from the dank rock fissure near the iron ladder that leads down the rock face to the river. Swimming quickly past, the sun warms my back till I meet the rapids and push into the flume. I sink slightly and whoosh down among the bubbles towards the luteous glow at the lower end of the pool.

GOODRINGTON
TO BROADSANDS
22 May

~

Another swim with Sophie today from Goodrington to Broadsands, near Paignton. It's hot and sunny and the sea is flat and warm; light splays off red sand, still wet from the retreating tide. It smells like summer. We swim face down through forests of weed, some of which stroke and pull at our limbs, while others scour like Brillos. A school of tiny, blue fish zip past, dodging through a mini-canyon.

As we approach Armchair Rock, the sea turns tepid as bathwater. Water ebbs and flows around curiously pitted and holed limestone formations with a sound like vindaloo-induced indigestion. Sophie wallows and exclaims, transfixed by the shapes and the sounds.

I venture a couple of short runs of butterfly, but it's difficult getting the timing back after my injury. Switching back to crawl I hit a thermocline where the water is suddenly icy, sending a shiver through my bare feet, hands and head.

Approaching Broadsands beach I feel and hear a strimmer-like sound cutting through me. I turn to see a couple of speed boats shooting across the bay, ejaculating sea water from their engines as they pass. It's a horrible return to the real world.

DOUBLE DART
24 May
~

I'm baking and sticky with sweat after the hottest day this year, and the sound and sight of the Double Dart as the air starts to cool makes me want to run flat out and dive straight in. We walk upstream and change among the trees. The river rocks are slippery, so our entrance is less nifty than we had hoped. As I fall forwards, the deliciously cool water sluices the heat and salt from my skin and I'm instantly invigorated.

We swim serenely around the pool, passed occasionally by a speeding dog; we have Honey and Perrin the labrador with us this evening. It's a joy to watch a dog bred for swimming cavorting through the river, water rilling from his coat.

We swim in each pool before plopping in to the Horseshoe jacuzzi. I feel the fizzling softness on my skin. Janey says the bubbles make happy water, and I know what she means. I hold a handful of bubbles briefly before they evanesce like Tinkerbell.

THE LYD
25 May
~

Dry heat rises in waves from the moorland track. Squadrons of skylarks take off from the gorse, dull brown, and rise slowly before suddenly letting rip, fluttering and singing their hearts out, higher and higher and higher.

It's a thrill to slip into Witch's Pool and wallow in amber water, surrounded by the tinkle of the falls and brushed by occasional gusts from a warm breeze. Honey rootles along the edge.

We jog down to the little cascade and I float face down in the sparkling flume. As I roll over, a kestrel flies directly overhead on arched wings. Two women seated on the Black Rock bench wave and smile at me while new beaming-yellow gorse flowers waft their exotic coconut scent.

BOVISAND
28 May

~

It's evening and the sun is low, flooding Bovisand with light reflected from sea, sky and wet sand. The inlet glows softly, guarded by dark rocks pointing out to Cornwall like dragon's feet.

Occasionally, the growl of a boat engine augments the reptilian grumble and crash of the sea. The breakwater appears to hover in a fairytale cloud. We bob around and leap through waves while gulls float nearby in puddles of light.

SALTER'S POOL
29 May

~

We met in the usual place and wandered up to Salter's Pool for a chilling-off after another hot and sunny day. Horseshoe Falls gave us a pummelling akin to trotting for ten miles bareback on a Dartmoor pony, and we were all bursting with bonhomie. Two latecomers arrived and leapt in with Queenie and Jane, while the rest of us dried off.

Then Jackie got the cake out.

The water in Salter's, previously black and smooth as Guinness, churned as though a carcass had been flung to a school of ravenous piranhas. Jackie stood on the bank and extended her cake-loaded hand. Jane and Queenie emerged from the scrum together, but a passing salmon staged a dazzling leap over their heads and grabbed the cake. Queenie executed a glorious dive, but lost control on the slithery rocks and smacked into Jane before they both plummeted back to the river, crushing the salmon beneath them. Jane grabbed the cake from the jaws of the stunned fish. Jackie, fearing for her fingers, lobbed a spare piece to Queenie.

As the sun set we scoffed the last of the cake and the churning waters subsided. The lifeless salmon floated downstream on her final journey, turning stiffly in the current, glinting silver through the dark water. Jane threw a mid-stream Falling Tree Pose in an attempt to pretend she had been calmly practicing yoga all along and had played no part in the tragic death of the salmon. A final shock-wave hit her, and she was tossed gracefully downstream like a branch in a winter storm.

BOVISAND
2 June

~

As is usual for Devon Moon Gazey swims, we drove to Bovisand through tipping rain and floods with windscreen wipers on double speed. I'm sure I saw the moon as a faint glow through the clouds, but it certainly wasn't gazeable. Sky and sea were the slaty-grey that soaks up light. A band of ripped seaweeds and shells mulled around in the shallows, but at least the rain had stopped. Several people had their toes nibbled, possibly by the famous Wembury Bay cuckoo wrasse. Who needs to pay for a fishy pedicure?

Gulls and a cormorant bobbed around and fished nearby. Walking from the water over wet sand, we left our footprints among those of the birds.

SHARRAH

6 June

~

Between summer storms Catherine, Gill, the dogs and I wend our way through squidgy mud and damp air to Sharrah. The river pounds and rumbles, and none of the lower pools are swimmable. We are hit by a grizzly roar where the waters are forced through the narrows above Bel Pool Island.

Sharrah boils burnt orange today, another colour I've not seen here before. A beery foam head floats atop the eddy and cakes our chins so we appear to have been caught mid-shave. My arms and legs glow the colour of a spray tan. Huge bubbles appear and process downstream, held above the surface by little foamy floats.

Swimming flat out into the beer head, I adjust my stroke so I can sweep it away from my face. It smells slightly off, like the whiff of an over-ripe cheese, but the water is beautifully cool and smooth and fresh as summer rain. Eddie the terrier is almost engulfed, while Socks the collie panics when she loses sight of one of us and emits a volley of alarm-barks. Honey drops yet another ball into the river and spends the swim trying to dig it up from between some tree roots.

I decide against braving the top of the rapid current and go in below the big rock. Even there I'm pushed under by a down-surge and get that helpless sinking feeling, where you know you can't float and just have to go with it; it's a reminder of how it feels not to be able to swim. The river spits me back up and I spin slowly in the current.

ODDICOMBE
10 June

~

Sophie Pierce and Matt Newbury gave a fascinating talk on the history of Wild Swimming in Torbay. Among many notable discoveries, Sophie and Matt had uncovered a cine film from the 1930s showing a group of local women executing perfect swallow dives from sixty-foot cliffs into the sea; a local diving champion and Olympian trained in the same spot. This practice has now been turned on its head to the criminalised feet-first jumping called 'tombstoning'.

Following the talk, we descended on the Cliff Railway to Oddicombe for a rainy, choppy swim. We frolicked into the water en masse through dumping waves, which resulted in some interesting shrieks.

The sea is a good degree or two colder than the moorland rivers at the moment. While I was mostly anaesthetised by the cold, I nevertheless felt a squidgy bump on the arm, which turned out to be a jellyfish. I wasn't alone, and one swimmer was stung on the face. A couple of us found our what-lies-beneath-the-water phobias resurfacing, the most common of which involved being nudged or mouthed by the infamous Torbay seal-with-the-sense-of-humour.

We had discussed on the way down the sewage outfall following the recent storms: swimming and bouncing through the brine I saw a white shape which I assumed to be a sanitary towel – Queenie and Stef laughed openly and informed me it was a cuttlefish. A reiteration of the power of suggestion on the mind, and of course I wasn't wearing my glasses.

LOWER SPITCHWICK
14 June

~

Cold, windy, dank and grey: summer on Dartmoor...

Faye and I enter the dark metallic waters of the Dart in the pool above the Cresta Run. Chilly shivers travel through my skin and I want to get out. Looking up, it's a shock to see the summer greens of ferns and trees. I force myself to swim, hating the creep of cold as my hair wicks water. Gusts of wind ruckle the surface as they pass. We clamber down the shallows towards the corner current and my body is picked up and flung along as I swoop round the bend.

MEWSTONE
16 June

~

The Mewstone – in this weather? Well, we tried.

It's blowing a hoolie and there's officially a six- to eight-foot swell. The Mewstone taunts us from the maelstrom, highlighted by spray from the surrounding reef; there's no way we'll make it there today. Most of the gang have failed to show, and John our safety-kayaker decides it's too frisky for him to paddle through the surf, so he opts instead to 'stay on the beach and photograph you guys drowning.' Sophie does some bodyboarding while JJ, Hugo and I go for a swim.

The water's warm and churning, and I dive through some of the waves as they break, they shoot up to the top so as to push and plummet off the back. I grin through the constant rumble and hiss of crashing waves and foam, imbued with stormy energy. As we swim beyond the surf, we hit the crazy choppy area where wind, tide and currents meet. We're walloped and whipped and flung. There's a whiff of sewage from the Point.

White horses break as we crest, and spindrift runs towards the shore in the squall that hits us around halfway to the Mewstone. Small wrinkles cover bigger ones in the gusting wind. Rain splats into my face and partially washes the sticky brine from my skin.

Slicks of uprooted weed marble the sea, and I hit one as I swim. It slows me and pulls at my arm. I'm breathing on the downwind side, swimming at an angle to the waves, and timing my breaths for the point where I feel myself dropping off the top. But this time I'm slapped in the face by a witch's hat wave just as I inhale; I cough salty water through my abraded throat for a couple of minutes before I can breathe again.

I decide to make my way to shore, while JJ and Hugo continue on for a few minutes. I keep my eye on the church and head back against the tide which is now retreating. I'm quite scared as I watch the backs of breakers rushing the beach; I know they're too strong for me to body-surf. I decide to swim hard and look behind as I breathe.

When a wave is about to break, its lip teeters before curling into a sneer, after which, like a school bully, it gets you. So: I stop, face it and dive underneath. They come at me fast in the breaking zone and it's hard, frantic work for a couple of minutes, with barely time to catch a breath between.

Suddenly I'm through, and I can surf in where the worst of the energy has dissipated. I stagger to the shore and look back to spot Hugo and JJ appearing. Hugo is wiped out by a huge wave, losing his prescription goggles while his body bends in ways it's not designed for.

The sun appears and lights the foaming surface so that it gleams like fish-skin.

TINSIDE
19 June

~

It's a sunny day with a nippy onshore breeze. Plymouth Hoe sparkles under the bright blue sky as I walk towards the railings.

And then it appears, the Art Deco joy that is Tinside Lido. Curving out over the sea, flags waving, fountain spewing from its centre: this isn't a normal swimming pool. Almost circular so you can swim in arcs rather than lengths, its rippled clear-filtered seawater is illuminated by the sun and refreshed by the sea breeze. We swim, dive and play before sitting on the concrete bench to warm and dry our chilled skin in the sun.

SPITCHWICK
26 June

~

Sundown. Honey and I crawl through the dismal Dartmoor landscape, drained and limp with the fog that has smothered us all day. As we descend into the Dart Valley our view is suddenly brighter. Above, a patch of blue appears through parting clouds; below is a watery world illuminated like a Medieval bible. We swim against the chill current and bathe in sunbeams which reflect and ripple across the rock face above us like a river of light.

NORTH TEIGN
30 June

~

We stride over Kes Tor on a blustery day with little bursts of rain, sun and scudding clouds. Honey jumps through a bog and snaps at the cotton tails as they bob back and forth in the gale. I glimpse the North Teign in the distance, narrow and straight as it crosses the common, and hear the tinkle of water despite the squelching of rain-sodden turf as we tread. My hair slaps across my face and even the hairs on my arms are blowing horizontally.

We cross the tiny clapper bridge and walk through foxgloves, thistles and bracken. Walla Brook joins the river as it begins its plummet into Teigncombe Cleave, just above a holey rock that sits above the water like a wild lavatory. My friend Jackie tells me this is the Whooping Cough Stone: if you pass a child suffering it through the hole, they will be cured.

We dip and swim in a lovely pool enveloped by mountain ash, blackthorn and gorse. As the sun comes out the water glows like a winter fire reflected in burnished copper, adding to the frisson of chill as I dunk under. I try to swim but keep grounding on submerged slabs slimy with brown silt. The wind swoops upstream and ruffles the surface which glints like a shoal of fish.

We wend our way back upstream past the pong of a dead sheep, her body dissolved like the Wicked Witch of the West beneath a splatted fleece and gently curving horns.

Upstream from the clapper bridge I float on my back in the shallows, water rushing one way and wind the other. Rushes and foxgloves bend like animal pelts in the wind. Bruise-grey clouds gather behind.

SUGARY COVE
1 July
~

Just around the corner from Dartmouth Castle, Sugary Cove is as sweet and lovely as it sounds.

The tide is high, and we enter the pale turquoise sea from rocks then swim along to the gully. Cliffs tower above while gulls wheel overhead. A pair of nesting oystercatchers rush past, black and white with long orange beaks, emitting frequent squeaky-toy calls. We dive down and see a large crab who quickly pulls a frond of seaweed over her shell like a wig in an attempt to disguise herself.

Around the corner, overlooked by the Castle, is a cave where we play for a while. The pale, quartz-veined slabs close to the surface make the water pulse with colour. We swim around the outside, where a gull guards a guano-iced rock and the oystercatchers reappear, circuiting us several times in alarm. The scent of seabird wafts over us, while white-sheeted yachts sail silently past like ghosts.

We find another deep cave on the opposite side of the bay. We're pulled in and shooshed back; it's like being caught in the windpipe of a living creature. The cold hits here under the damp and limpeted walls.

We swim back to shore in sunshine through fragments of weed suspended in bright sea.

TAVY CLEAVE
5 July

~

It's not raining, so we head off to Tavy Cleave to find a dipping spot and discover a lovely little pool below a shallow cascade overlooked by steeply-pointed Ger Tor. Just below the falls, Honey and I slip into water the colour of ginger cake made with black treacle. I barely notice the chill, and the scent of sheep fades as I dip under. The cascade roars and the birds sing while the wind blusters. I swim against the current, adjusting my stroke as the flow buffets me in order to stay in the same place, and watch a bird of prey hover over the escarpment, jinking in the wind to a similar end.

I float back down past a ginormous Dartmoor slug, black and wrinkled like slightly animated fox poo. A slow-worm slides away, beautiful in shades of taupe and cappuccino with just enough iridescence to stay on the right side of tasteful. The bird of prey, a sparrowhawk I think, swoops down and vanishes.

SHARRAH
11 July

~

Honey and I squidge up to Sharrah just as the sun begins to make tentative appearances. It's a bright, juicy green everywhere after weeks of rain, and we're walloped with the usual crescendo and energy surge as we cross the stile above the lower rapids. The pool is black, and the currents are patterned with fine foam like paisley fabric.

Today, I swim through water like iced black coffee, silver bubbles trailing from my hands and mouth. The upper cascade foams and sprays and I float face down through ginger-ale fizz. I have ice-cream neck, but it soon passes. I practice my strokes heading upstream and feel the current pressing against my arms and body; I try to streamline myself but the water direction is too random. Floating on my back, I watch wisps of white wander across a slice of bright blue sky.

PLYMOUTH HOE
12 July

~

We meet for a Thursday evening swim on Plymouth Hoe after yet another hideous day of torrential rain, wind and mist. Unusually, the boys outnumber the girls. We pick our way over rocks and seaweed into murky greeny-grey water. The wind slaps rain over me and I chill instantly so that the sea feels almost warm. Drake's Island and a cruise ship loom in and out of view through the fog.

The minute I hit the water I feel better. The spray sparks off my burning skin and I smell stormy sea. Every so often patches of slender weed wrap my limbs like bony fingers in a ghost train. I bump around randomly enjoying the sensation of being slapped by frantic waves. The wind roars in my ears enhancing the feeling of a fairground ride.

I swim and concentrate on holding my glide while I breathe, allowing the sea to dictate an erratic rhythm. I roll with the white horses and wait, sneaking breaths where I can see a gap in the slapping waves. We swim back in and are dumped inelegantly among the shingle, weed and sand on the shore.

CRAZYWELL POOL
21 July

~

Crazywell Pool is overflowing down the Gurt, smooth and black and – according to local legend – deeper than the combined length of the bell ropes from Walkhampton Church. We swim through opaque water, the cloudy sky reflected in its rippled surface. There is a layer of warmth on top, but the depths are cooler, catching dangling feet and hands. Crossing the centre of the pool, I swim above the spring and am iced by a wintry blast while the sun sneaks through and warms my head.

LOSTWITHIEL
TO GOLANT
22 July

~

Early morning, bright sunshine. The water in the upper reaches of the tidal Fowey river is a chilly 12.5 degrees and I'm glad of my wetsuit.

Stef and I have decided to pootle for this cheeky little four-mile swim, and once we've warmed up we stop for a float and chat, washed with green light from overhanging trees. We meander with the river, its banks frayed by masses of reeds, and pass a pair of unconcerned swans while skeins of Canada geese cross overhead. A swallow swoops close enough to touch.

The water is thick and opaque with silty lifeforms, illuminated by distinct rays of greeny-amber. I watch the bubbles stream from my hands and hear the glug as I exhale. Floating on my back, sun sprays from ripples. The river widens, and there's a faint tang of saltiness like perspiration.

Now we are able to stand, feet sliding in clay studded with harder nuggets. I'm ambushed by Stef and Richard and we lob mud pies at each other. Queenie (towing a dry-bag full of cake), Rosie and Bridget mud jump to meet us, bouncing along through waist-high water in a slow-mo run like Chariots of Fire. The estuary is wide, littered with boats, and overwhelmingly blue.

PLYMOUTH HOE
& DARTMEET
24 July
~

Such a glorious day, so I decided to go for a double dip.

This morning I swam a mile along Plymouth Hoe. The city's finest were out in force, and I changed near a gang of blokes swigging White Lightning from three-litre bottles, smoking, swearing at each other, and commenting on passing women's breasts. Luckily, I don't have any of those...

I swam out past the lido and was overtaken by a pilot-boat and then a frigate making a huge racket, presumably on her way back from a detachment. My next encounter was with the 'One Hour Plymouth Tour' boat dropping off one lot of passengers and reloading another. I waited for them to pass, feeling rather like an exotic fish in the aquarium as people pointed at me and exclaimed (I hope because I was wearing my new loud swimsuit).

As I swam back across the buoy-marked swimming area (limit 4kts) the drunk blokes swept past at full speed in two boats with in-boards, shaking their tails, enveloping me with a smog of exhaust fumes and almost drowning me in their wake. A boy belonging to the gang threw stones at a little girl in the shallows, calling her no end of names, while the adults chugged more cider and shouted at each other. The overall impression was of the kind of uncivilised wildness I'd rather avoid.

Late afternoon, I wandered up the East Dart from Dartmeet. Most people here confine themselves to a picnic next to the car, but just a little way upstream is a lovely dipping pool sheltered by oaks, one of which appears to be executing a theatrical bow: *Come in, come in*, it seems to say.

This is an altogether nicer experience. The water glistens amber and green and feels like satin. I share the pool with some kids who show me how their swimming shorts blow up underwater, while my friend JJ sits like a Dartmoor Pixie on the rocks having gashed his arm and been banned from the wet.

HORNDON CLAM
26 July
~

Spent the day on tenterhooks while Queenie and JJ slogged through their epic Channel swim. They left Dover just after 2am but following seasickness and extreme cold they were forced to stop around thirteen hours later, just three miles from their goal. In awe of their courage, stamina and strength.

Feeling devastated for my friends, I set off with Honey to Horndon Clam on the river Tavy, near where we live. Clambering down the track, we take the tiny path upstream from the Clam through the woods, going past twisty oaks, luscious bracken and orchids. The fields on the far side are edged with Dartmoor's bunting of barbed wire hung with sheep's wool.

It's still baking hot. I feel sweat prickling my skin and every so often there's a sharp itch where a cleg fly bites. Honey and I dip by the little falls, cleansed by sparkling bubbles which seem to release stress as they burst. They're silver at the surface where the sun catches them, fading to pale amber in deeper water.

We walk back and slide into the deep pool. It's black and still, soaked with reflected colour. I float downstream so as not to disturb the calm, then swim back up. The current is almost invisible here until I swim against it and the water pushes over my face and shoulders.

A pair of wrens watch from low down in a tree and fly off trilling as Honey shakes the water from her coat.

BANTHAM
4 August
~

Queenie, Kate, Honey and I drive down to Bantham at nightfall for our Moon Gazey swim. A faint smudge of light through the clouds on the horizon behind us, like a distant glow-worm, raises our hopes of the moon putting in an appearance.

There's enough light to feel the shapes of the dunes and I sense the sea before I see it, swelling like molten pewter. It's high tide so the earlier surf has died down to a gentle swell, which is just as well since there are rips here. Kate sets up her chair on the beach while the rest of us strip in the chill air, splattered by occasional rain drops. We trot naked to the sea. The sand is damp and hard beneath my feet and the cool breeze tickles my salty skin.

We wade in over smooth kelp. The water creeps up my body like an incipient shiver; the shushing of distant breakers swirls around in the breeze so that sound and sensation are indistinguishable. I learned recently that the music of waves is created by thousands of bubbles of air which vibrate and ring underwater like little bells. I feel the bubbles ring through my skin as I swim, and phosphorescence sparks from my arms. We are mesmerised and wave our arms through the water with fingers splayed. Ducking under with eyes open, I see green glints blossom like tiny neon lights seen through a rain-blurred window.

We're quite far out, floating between sea and sky. As we turn back, the moon creeps above the clouds and illuminates a trembling, silvery path to the shore.

AVETON GIFFORD
TO BANTHAM
11 August
~

On escort duty today for a group swim down the beautiful Aune. There are swans with cygnets around, and someone has added Beware Mad Swan in marker pen at the bottom of the car park sign in Aveton Gifford.

Blue sky with mackerel clouds and bright sun make the river water glow greeny-orange. As it's a neap tide, we have to walk a bit more than usual through squidgy mud and shallow water – all part of the wild swimming experience!

As I swim, mud seamlessly gives way to sand and shells; tufts of sea lettuce point the way. I taste a tang of salt, then feel the chill on my feet and hands where the denser seawater has sunk beneath the warm blanket of the river. The underwater landscape is pocked with coiled ragworm casts like tiny Inca temples. A large fish crosses beneath me, but I have no idea what species it is. The easterly wind hits as we round the bend near the village. The current from the receding tide is breathtaking here, and where it runs fastest the breeze has whipped the water to a frenzy.

We stop briefly, then decide to swoop down with the current, exiting before the rip pulls us out to sea. Many of our swimmers haven't done this kind of thing before, but all of them are game and trust me! We shoot past the summer holiday world of the sand bar on the corner; it's littered with people laughing and enjoying the sun, in stark contrast to the wild isolation upstream.

We exit at the estuary mouth; a sparkling vision of rough water, blowing spray and sunlight, through which Burgh Island hovers in the distance like Avalon.

SHARRAH
12 August
~

We meet up with some visiting wild swimmers from Dorset to show off the enchanted jewel of Devon wild swims, Sharrah Pool. The sun has fought through the clouds by the time we arrive; the river's surface sparkles above amber shallows and dark depths. A dipper flashes by.

The water is noticeably chilly. Once acclimatized, I dive under, swimming along the bottom through an aquascape of tumbled rocks and saffron silt.

The two boys with us are grinning, effervescent as the bubbles they swim through. Their mum is perched on the edge of the cascade like the Birth of Venus. We float and shoot the rapids, swim upstream, and sun ourselves on rocks. A beautiful demoiselle darts around the bank, flashing deep turquoise.

The Sharrah virgins are predictably entranced.

75

SHARRAH

15 August

~

The morning deluge is long gone, but the moorland rivers are still rising at teatime when we meet. Kayaks are spread around the car park, a rare sight in the summer. We peer over the parapet as we cross New Bridge and it scares us. Walking up through mud and dripping trees, we hear the river seethe; it's creamy with foam and the colour of dark chocolate. Parts of the path have fallen away over the summer with the constant rain.

Foam maps the movement of water in Sharrah pool, and there's an eddy I haven't seen before on the far side; the current from the cascade reaches three-quarters of the way down, and the eddy circles in a spiral back up the far bank, like stirred coffee. Usually, there are rock-studded shallows at the lower end of the pool where you drift gently aground before the river is forced in a rapid through the narrows, but today the surge completely covers the rocks and there's a real danger of being swept over. No swimmer would survive that trip. The water is relatively still at the near bank below the entry spot, and we decide we can safely return and exit here. I scan the river for fallen trees, but it looks clear.

We enter the beautiful, chill river and swim with difficulty upstream. It's like being jostled in a mosh pit; arms and legs are bashed in different directions while our bodies vibrate with the roaring bass notes of the falls. I whack my foot on a rock, having not realised I'd been pushed so far over. We collect foam quiffs and moustaches on the way up to the big boulder where we are able to balance and experience the upper cascade. The energy suffuses me, spray and surging water pulse in time with my blood. I dive forwards and feel like a dolphin in the boiling chocolate water, sinking now and again as I lose my buoyancy.

76

I return to the top, but this time stay longer with the flume, trying to enter the circular eddy. I'm ripped past, and have to swim out to escape to the near bank, my body bending like a banana.
I'm panting with effort and exhilaration. Huge raindrops hit my head, and I float on my back in the eddy while the rain forms little fountains on the surface and the oak overhead bends and rustles its leafy tambourine in the gale.

We barbecue in the rain, talk, and drink wine and beer. A couple of kayakers stop for a chat on their way past. We wander back through the pitch-black woods well after nightfall. The foam on the surface of the river glows and illuminates its passage down the dark gorge.

PLYMOUTH HOE
19 August

~

I don't usually do organised swims, but it's really not possible to swim from the Breakwater to Plymouth Hoe without some serious official planning, thanks to all the ships, cross-channel ferries and submarines which pass through.

We left by boat from the Mayflower Steps and motored out in sunshine over dead calm seas. You could practically smell the testosterone from the serious swimmers, who flexed their muscles and discussed their planned split times. I swim on a different planet!

We jumped ship close to the Breakwater, above which peeped the Mewstone some two miles from the finish point next to Tinside Lido. The sea was balmy and opaque with mashed seaweed from the recent storm. I got into the zone, aware only of the bubbling sound of my exhalation and flashes of landmarks as I inhaled.

The sun warmed the left side of my face. Every so often I pulled my head up to see my spotting points of Smeaton's Tower and the big wheel. They seemed to stay as tiny dots for ages before suddenly growing as I neared the Hoe.

Approaching the yellow buoy, I realised my line was off and felt the current pushing me to the east. I adjusted my course and swam harder but was being swept fast away from the finish towards the Plym. I was forced to swim the last twenty minutes in top gear. The previously yogic, steady bubbling of my exhalations became a walrus-type snorting and I imagined other swimmers panicking as they wondered what horrible sea monster was approaching.

Finally, I felt the bottom grow nearer and my hands brushed the sand. I looked up to see a packed beach, and staggered ashore. We swimmers were all wearing facial algae which resembled gingery brown five o'clock shadows, and my voice had dropped an octave thanks to a sore throat from the salt water; I could easily have secreted myself among the bewhiskered folk singers on the terrace.

MEL TOR POOL
20 August

~

Stef, Honey and I wander up past Sharrah towards Mel Tor Pools.

As we pick our way through the undergrowth, Stef exclaims and points: 'A cormorant!'. I'm slightly confused, thinking she must mean a heron. I look again and perched on a rock in midstream is, indeed, a rather handsome specimen. He throws a few poses as we creep up on him, cameras at the ready, and begins then to vibrate his throat and exercise his impressive hooked beak. Stef tells me about her friend who had his hand badly lacerated by one while swimming wearing a wetsuit; the bird probably mistook it for a fish. She puts her hands in her pockets.

We check our cormorant over; although they do come inland, I've never seen one this far from the coast. He doesn't look unwell or injured and is apparently sunbathing. These birds look black in the sea, but here I can pick out his beautiful grey and tan plumage, his orange 1960s lipstick, and the fish-scale markings on his wings. Eventually, having worked through his full repertoire of improbable yogic poses, he flies casually upstream.

We dump our kit on the bank and wade across the river in swimsuits and bare feet. The water is pretty heavy and Honey struggles to stay away from the cascade, so I have to keep grabbing her. We make it across and scramble up to the main pools over squidgy leaf mould, stopping often to remove holly leaves from our feet.

The water proves too high, so we climb back and shoot with the current down the long pool. Our cormorant, who I think I shall name Livingstone, is again perched on his rock; as we approach he flies off, downstream this time.

We stop to play at Sharrah on the way back. A couple of yellow-banded dragonflies swoop overhead, bright against the blue sky. On the far bank, where the gorge rises sheer above the river, is a small grotto where water still pours after the recent rain. It drips from the hanging vegetation, while light splays from the river's surface and reflects in dancing ripples on the wet rock. Beautiful desmoiselle damselflies scoot above the glowing amber water in the sunlight, metallic wings flashing. A yellow wagtail bobs on a rock nearby.

MEWSTONE
26 August
~

We finally arrange a circumnavigation of Mewstone on a day when the weather and sea conditions are relatively good. There's a bit of an onshore breeze, a two- to three-foot swell and good visibility. I had planned the swim based on advice from Dave Curno, a yachtsman with an encyclopedic knowledge of tides and currents around the area who had given us a talk a few weeks back. He suggested we should swim anticlockwise at high tide plus three hours, when the apparently random currents should be at their most accommodating. It's a serious swim out to sea, to an island which sits out in the channel tidal stream in deep water. This picture is complicated by the funnelling effect of the Plymouth Breakwater, the Yealm estuary current, and the shallow narrows between the Mewstone and Wembury Point.

We set out for the famous island accompanied by four kayaks. It's a hard swim into breeze and the chop, and there is a strange illusion by which the Mewstone appears to get further away like a ship dragging its anchor, before growing suddenly closer and touchable. Jess and I arrive shortly after Queenie and Jo, while Max and Marisa the two racing eels are already heading around the back. We spot a huge cave and swim over but it's not accessible at this water level, though it looks ripe for exploration on a higher tide.

Cormorants pose with beaks to the sky, jagging the silhouette of the cliff, and gulls wheel overhead. We head up the western side of the island which is striped in horizontal waves of nut brown, black and grey-green, topped by a crenelated and tussocky hillock. It looks like the body of a cuddly jellyfish, not at all what I was expecting.

Approaching the seaward side, we are hit by some sizeable swell. From our low-level view we see the tops of sails leaning into the wind, and then a jet-black shard of rock like a shark's fin thrusting from the sea at an angle of forty-five degrees. Waves splat and rush up the flat surface, foaming back down. The sea is petrol blue and turbulent, and we feel nervous without a kayak in view. We press on because the current between the Mewstone and Wembury Point from whence we came is fast and flowing out to sea.

Buffeted and bounced, our view ranges from water only, to the crews and decks of the nearby yachts, to the tops of their sails. In the other direction is the rest of the sinister, shattered rock slab, looking like a Gothic cathedral plummeting to hell. Waves crash and boom. I catch a distant glimpse of white water which marks the position of the reef to the Yealm side. These lethal rocks are named The Slimers and we want to avoid them. I've seen the gully between them and the island on Google Earth and Dave has told us there should be two metres of water there at this time. He's right, and we swim over weed and rocks with plenty of water to spare. I'm panting with the effort of swimming so hard; it's too strong a sea in which to relax.

Here a ridge rises steeply at an angle like the spine of a stegosaurus, and secreted in the hollow towards its base is a small stone building incorporating a roundhouse. The spine and the cottage are washed on their seaward side with yellowy-green lichen. This must have been the home of the infamous prisoner of the Mewstone, who chose banishment here in preference to deportation in the nineteenth century. I wonder how this hasn't been sold as an ideal second home renovation project for an investment banker, like pretty much every other vernacular Devon building.

81

We exit the gully and are momentarily confused. I spot Wembury Church in the far distance and realise we were about to head for Plymouth. Then Lindsay and Claire materialise on the horizon in their kayaks like bedraggled sea angels to escort us back in.

The waves are mostly with us, and we should be able to swim easily but it's a struggle. I've lost my rhythm, am very tired, and starting to get cramp in one calf and the other hamstring.

Consciously relaxing, I manage to shake it out. It's impossible to glide because of the buffeting so I have to grit my teeth and go for it. My mouth and throat are raw with salt water, and my tongue is stuck to the roof of my mouth. I dream of my water bottle back on the shore and swim harder. Breathing to the left, I realise the Yealm current has pushed me over towards the Point so have to swim at an angle into it to get round the rocks to the beach.

Finally I see pale sand, and surf in on two tiny waves. I'm greeted by cheers from some of our friends who came for a little swim and waited for us. The adventure has taken the faster pair around one hour and forty minutes, but we've been nearer two and a half. I have just enough energy left to do a little dance on the beach.

SHARRAH
12 September

~

Early evening on a misty, drizzly autumnal day. No glorious sunset, just a patch of glowing white between pewter clouds that look heavy enough to sink with the sun. We creep in to water that manages to be both clear and the colour of an oil slick. The bottom is softly carpeted with fallen vegetation. Midges nip at our faces.

The river is very chilly indeed; I swim as hard as I can upstream to heat up. Finally, I'm suffused with a warm glow which starts in my bones and seeps through to my skin. Bats flitter past, flashes of dark above black water. The last notes of birdsong fade into the night.

BURGH ISLAND
23 September

~

A day after the Outdoor Swimming Society's Dart 10k, we have about thirty swimmers from around the country excited at the prospect of an iconic Devon wild swim. I've never swum Burgh Island in an easterly gale before, but I see from the cliffs that it's doable. We walk down past the sea tractor and into warm, pale turquoise sea.

The water is miraculously clear; I can see finally the cheese grater rock that once scraped a piece from my thigh. I'm exhilarated by the wild energy of the storm and the towering cliffs and wonder whether we'll get into Death Valley. The entrance looks spookily calm; I watch for a bit before deciding it's safe to enter.

My companion and I swim in, joined quickly by several others who've been hovering to see whether we would survive. We swim through the outer reef towards the shelter of the cliffs.

Suddenly I'm in a cauldron of pointed wavelets about a foot high, spiralling like upside down tornadoes. Spray flies from their tops. There's an invisible wizard somewhere, casting spells over the sea.

Every few yards the surface of the water transmogrifies: here are sharp waves that echo the shapes of the jagged rocks above; there, tiny ruffles shiver across rounded swells; a splatter of rain-pocked wavelets; white horses rear with manes of spindrift. It's still somehow clear below the surface, and we dive down through waving weeds.

We play our way through the rocks to where the sandbar is gradually revealed by the receding tide. The gale hits us full force, flinging abrasive water as it rips through. There's no big swell, just a wallop of wavelets that makes swimming hard. I'm battered side to side and front to back but keep my head down. As we leave the water, I freeze instantly from the chill of the east wind.

BUGLE HOLE
24 September
~

We're not sure exactly where this natural tidal pool is, but as we descend the cliff path Bugle Hole reveals itself. We scramble down and change on rocks the texture of fossilised Cadbury's Flakes. I squat on the edge and the sea surges up to meet me so that I'm snatched from damp autumnal air into water.

The sea beyond us is churning and spraying in the gale, but we're mostly protected by a rock wall resembling the top of a portcullis. From time to time a big wave foams through a gap like saliva from the mouth of a crocodile contemplating a juicy swimmer. I float over to explore the top of a narrow cave which is also a blow hole in the right conditions; it sucks me in and spits me out.

On the other side is a narrow gully connected to the sea, through which the swell is forced. It's a topsy-turvy world where the landscape is hidden and revealed randomly; from bouncing in deep water you suddenly find yourself stranded atop a rock with the water surface three feet below. Honey is bemused.

I swim from the shelter of the Hole as the sun breaks through. Emerge into a glittering sea.

SCAREY TOR
26 September
~

Heavy rain, water pouring from the hills, beer-head foam. Cullever Steps is not swimmable today, so I slip into the little pool below Scarey Tor. I mean to push hard off the underwater rocks and cross the flood to an eddy on the far side, but the rock I stand on is like glass and I slide straight in and under the central cascade. I almost go over the edge, but somehow make it across. I'm laughing as I bob in the nippy water which is black as stewed tea. I return with more success and grab the top of a rock to pull myself out. Standing on sodden turf, rain needles my body through the cold afterglow. White mist winds itself along Belstone ridge.

MELDON POND
6 October
~

Meldon Pond is a flooded limestone quarry around one hundred and thirty feet deep.

We cross the clam over the dark and flooded West Okement and squelch through the woods. Suddenly, through autumn trees illuminated by bright sun, a delicious, blue pool materialises. It's as though a chunk of sky has dropped down to stun us in this world of amber waters and green turf.

The leaves are starting to turn, and their greens and golds are mirrored around the edges of the pool, refracting their tints through the water so the ocean colours turn with them and become autumnal. The sky is a bright, cool blue and fish-boned with diaphanous clouds. I feel the nip of autumn in the air and the burn of clear, cold water on my skin.

A wall of rock like a fairytale castle teeters over us as we swim. The luminous grey is smooth and streaked with limestone trails that are almost indistinguishable from the ripples reflected off the surface of the pool. Ivy trails down. Our two new wild swimmers are enchanted, and so are we.

SLAPTON
6 October
~

A coterie of wild swimmers gather in late afternoon on Slapton Sands. It's a stunning day, but a cheeky easterly wind knifes through skin and bone as we trot to the sea. The waves rear up and dump in a clattering roar, and the shingle tinkles like rain as the waves recede. Jackie is wiped out and emerges bedraggled, but bravely continues to bounce in the aquamarine swell. Black-backed gulls wheel overhead.

We return to shore and take turns to soak in the portable wood-fired hot tub placed here for the day. 'Hot tub' is way too prosaic a term for such a marvel; it's an experience of extreme contrasts. The little attached woodburner heats seawater which magically wafts through a pipe into the tub. It's the same water in which we've just swum, yet it's a different animal. Heat diffuses through our chilled skin. Meanwhile the salty Slapton gale whips past our faces. The briny scent mingles with whiffs of woodsmoke. We wallow and giggle, cooking slowly while we drink champagne, eat a series of exceptional cakes, and finish with coffee and Baileys.

Honey stares with deep concentration at our cake, but her love of water – fortuitously – does not extend to baths. The sun drops and silhouettes the spa chimney, while the spray from the surf mists the horizon. Looking seawards it's like an infinity pool. Finally, I have to let someone else in. Leaping from the tub I dash for my robe and manage to change before the gale steals the warmth from my body.

LADRAM BAY
7 October
~

We descend the hill through an ugly rash of caravans and blue signs pointing out everything from Swimming Pool to Caravan Sales. We reach the slipway and halt ahead of the NO DOGS sign. According to several websites dogs are allowed here, and Max, Michelle and I have chosen this place partly for this reason. We walk Frankepedo and Honey along the cliff path instead. A man with a Midlands accent rudely tells Michelle to put well-trained and innocent Frankie on the lead. The dogs are returned to the cars before we swim.

There are numerous people wandering around the caravan park, but there are only two others on the beach and the sea in the area below the slip smells of poo. This is not dog shit, but the result of untreated human sewage outfalls following recent heavy rain. I can accept dog bans on some popular beaches in summer, but this is ridiculous. A fledgling gull huddles into the shingle; presumably she's trying to avoid being banned too.

We edge out through painfully large pebbles into water that's murky with red sand. We swim over bumpy waves into a maelstrom of wild seas between the fabulous sandstone stacks, which are filled with holes like Hobbit Houses. It's stunning and lifts my spirits. Luckily, you can't see from here the visual effluent of caravans.

DEAD MAN'S CAVE
14 October

~

After days of deluge it's sunny and clear. We scramble over the rocks at low tide into refreshing, Mediterranean-blue sea.

Kari has a plan to swallow dive from the peak by the beach, in a tribute to beautiful photos of 1930s Torbay women we've seen, but the rock thrusts skywards like a warrior's statue, and the water below is mined with barnacled boulders which will be invisible at high tide.

We didn't swim much today; our progress was more a series of aquamarine wanderings.

Beneath the jagged limestone arch, I dive and find hundreds of starfish dotted around; warm yellow through the turquoise water, they have a Van Gogh look. Sue tells us that Dead Man's Fingers are more properly termed sea squirts. We decide that these splendid, multifarious specimens should be renamed Dead Man's Testicles or, as Kari suggests, sea bollocks.

It's a neap tide and we can see a slash of sun through the cliffs. The sea glows petrol blue and swells before pulling us into the light in a heavenly, near-death experience. We emerge close to the corner cave, and swim in through a trail of taupe scum and fronds of seaweed from the recent storms. I ponder why anyone should want to paint their home in taupe when they could choose aquamarine or starfish yellow.

The cave narrows. Rough ginger rocks are splattered with debris resembling strips of flesh. We are pushed up into the narrowing gap with the rise of the sea. I dive down and snake through the ribbon of blue; my claustrophobia disperses. Strange how not being able to breathe is comfortable when immersed in such beauty. We burst out beneath the arch; it feels like emerging from a wardrobe after a trip to Narnia.

SALTER'S POOL
22 October
~

The air's not that cold, but the water nips then burns like horseflies. It's dead calm, and autumn colours mist the trees. Lazy bright leaves wend downstream in the copper-black water. As I swim my breath condenses and creeps along the surface like a spectral breeze. I float across the current and my body swirls around and down towards the distant cascade; its music surges like rainfall as I pass.

Honey fossicks under the bank behind hanging tree roots like giant ribs so that she appears to have been swallowed by a fossilised whale.

WEMBURY
29 October
~

Dark clouds begin to glow as the moon staggers above. It's hard to judge the height of the surf as we wade into water the colour of lead; you don't see approaching breakers, but rather sense a looming presence. Wave lips flash with spray. A couple are big enough to have to duck under, while others break into our faces as we jump. My legs are grabbed by glossy kelp which slides down my thighs like a drowning bogeyman. The ghosts of waves fizzle on the surface before vanishing. Honey howls from the beach – it's too rough for her to swim with us and she's on the lead.

Moonlight glints off tipsy wavelets and silhouettes Wembury Church, and the lights of the Old Mill look like the orange eyes of a Halloween pumpkin. I levitate up waves in the dark then plummet, watching their speeding backs, then turning to glimpse the darkly distant shark's fin of the Mewstone. My skin is alive and burning with salty chill. Mesmerised by the moon, I gaze as a curl of cloud breaks over her face.

MELDON POND

4 November

~

Pauline, Queenie and a few others are aiming to swim at the Cold Water event in Tooting Bec Lido in January. To qualify they need to swim at 6 degrees for one kilometre wearing only a swimsuit and hat, so we tried Meldon Pond which – spring-fed and around 135 feet deep – is not known for its warmth.

It's chilly and mainly overcast. Once again, Meldon Dam is in full overflow and the Okement River rages beneath the leaf-spattered clam bridge as we cross. There are four dogs with us today: Honey, Max the springer, Maggie the spollie, and a Border terrier whose name I've forgotten. They cavort, leaping in then charging out, unleashing squeals and shrieks from swimmers in various states of undress whom they spray with rain storms of pond water.

The water feels freezing, and my limbs are almost immediately numbed before glowing bright red and burning. It takes five or six goes before I can swim front crawl and bear the chill on my cheekbones.

Nearing the quarried cliff at the far end, I'm struck by the contrast with the rest of the pond which is surrounded by semi-skeletal trees clinging to their remaining leaves. The wind shivers the grey surface of the water and elicits similar responses in my skin. Below the cliff, the light reflects from gleaming white lime trails and turquoise water. Vines dangle. My brain is confused by the frigid burning and the surreal view; it could be tropical, or it could be Arctic.

Afterwards, glowing cherry-red with my cold-water tan, I pull off my neoprene gloves and boots to expose luminous white hands and feet.

PLYMOUTH HOE
14 November

~

Mid-November, late afternoon and the sun is bright and low. The sea's nippy with a little chop and coloured dark blue-green. I get in quick and feel the unpleasant crawl of cold water up my body and an ache in my neck. I swim staccato for a minute or two, then the effect melds into the kind of sensation I imagine you'd have after a massage from a beefy Scandinavian using salt and willow switches. We swim round past the Lido, drift and bob and smile in the sunshine for a bit, then plough back against the wind and tide. If it weren't for the bracing chill it could be July – except in July it was like November.

SHARRAH
16 November

~

Jackie, Honey and I wander through dank woods and mist to Sharrah Pool. The deep water is slow and black; splatters of orange and yellow still cling to the trees.

The pool is less cold than we were expecting, so we swim gently upstream in water the colour of an old penny; its usual paisley pattern of foam is accented by fallen leaves. The rapids glow the colour of urine. All about is a blueish mist, heavy and veiled, through which the woods burn with autumn flames.

BEESANDS
9 December

~

Heaps of tanned pebbles add percussion to our footsteps as we walk to the sea which is gin clear and dead calm. Babette's boys are already frolicking like seals. I wade in and feel the nip as the water creeps up my body. The seabed is steeply shelving, and I swim straight away, the back of my neck contracting and shortening my stroke.

Beesands is a bleak and haunted place with a widescreen horizon, like the setting for a seaside Spaghetti Western. We laugh openly as Babette's non-outdoor-swimming friends walk in slow motion to their icy nemesis as though to a gunfight, bodies shrinking and faces contorting with the chill.

BURGH ISLAND
16 December

~

There's a point at which wild swimming becomes dangerous, and as a swimmer who loves the exhilaration and challenge of wild water it's vital I understand where that point is. Our risk-averse culture is anathema to me, and I can't think of anything worse than a life half-lived through fear and avoidance of perceived dangers, especially when statistically the riskiest thing most of us do is travel by car.

The swell today is forecast to be between eight and fourteen feet, and despite this a small gang of us want to swim round Burgh Island while the others dip or explore the Mermaid Pool. Although the circumnavigation looks doable from the shore, you can never sense the scale of the sea till you're in it.

There's a squall as we change and charcoal slashes of rain belt from bruised clouds. JJ and Ninja have swum early and we're looking out for them but there's no sign. Then they materialise and tell us they turned back because they were rolled head over heels by a pair of massive opposing waves, well away from any breaks. JJ, always on the crazy side of sensible, says it would be 'reckless' to try the swim which makes all but Hugo and me decide against it.

Swimming out to have a look won't be a problem – after all we've done this in big seas with far stronger winds before – so Hugo and I head out anticlockwise on the low spring tide. We know that the swell is from the south-west, and if we get that far we can use that energy on the home strait. This is the kind of adventure I love; the abrasive cold of the sea, the smell of stormy water with the whip of the wind on my skin, and the feeling of being on the edge of control.

We're bounced and buffeted and dropped from the backs of the waves. Stopping to chat, we're feeling good so decide to swim on for a few more minutes before reassessing. I film my swim for a minute and decide definitely not to go all the way round. Hugo's way ahead of me though, so I carry on hoping to catch him up. I'm still pretty comfortable.

There's an instant where it changes. I'm teetering fifteen feet up, and the rollercoaster thrill of the descent is punched from me by a side-on psycho wave. I'm lifted again at once and I peer towards where I last saw Hugo; on the pinnacle of the next swell there's a brief flash of his blue hat circled by a halo of spray and he's vanished into the Himalayan sea. My shouts are whipped away and buried beneath the avalanche roar of water meeting rocks and the distant shore. Now I'm lost, afraid and unsure, but know I should stay with Hugo. I swim towards him for a few strokes, but my breathing rhythm has gone and with it my stroke. I feel close to hyperventilating and know with utter certainty I have to turn back now.

A wave sweeps me up from behind and begins to break while a flood of adrenaline washes through my body. I force myself to breathe steadily and stare at the back of the wave racing away, glinting steel and with spray flying from the top. The friendly green-blue light has been sucked from the wavelets, and I'm struggling in a sinister, pewter darkness. Sandwiched between opaque sea and heavy slate sky, in my head I'm sinking. My legs are jellyfish as I try to swim, but I'm wearing my wetsuit for the first time since August and am unused to the buoyancy which pushes my head under while my legs fly up behind. The reef is almost within reach to my right; I could get over there but that thought shatters with the slow-motion crash of sea into rock. Struggling away from land, my fear tries to propel me back; I stop, bob for a bit and turn onto my back while I grapple with my breathing and pull myself together. I know I won't sink, but my left brain is saying otherwise. I float and think.

It's a waste of time doing breaststroke; I'm only trying because I want to see what's coming at me, but that's making me turn my head and stiffen up. I need to swim in front crawl towards the shore and trust myself. An apparition of Kari the mermaid muse tells me I don't need to look at the sea, I need to feel it, so I hold my glide, blowing a steady stream of bubbles underwater and waiting for gaps in the waves to inhale. I feel weightless and unmoving in the current as the water from the shore breakers sucks back out, as though in a disturbing dream where you want to wake but can't. There's a gap between the surf dashing towards the beach and the maelstrom around the island reefs. I head for it.

Suddenly it's over; the sea is smaller and lighter, and I can see the warm, golden sand of the neck. I keep going till I feel my hands brush the bottom, then stand and wade backwards while spent breakers tug at my legs. After a couple of worrying minutes, I spot Hugo ploughing towards me. As we trot across the beach he tells me about a mountaineer scaling Annapurna who dropped his gloves and had to watch them slide away, resulting in the loss of his fingers; Hugo says he too has had an 'Annapurna moment' today. We should have stayed with the others, of course.

BURGH ISLAND
24 December

~

We return to Burgh for a Christmas Eve swim in the hope of getting round the island this time. The swell is less, but it's much windier than forecast. I feel dull and spaced out having had just

95

three hour's sleep after a run of night shifts. We boing in through the surf and are whipped and bashed and smashed in the face by spray. My spirits lift with the swell and I realise that my teeth are chilled because I'm smiling under the water.

Bouncing along, we chat and laugh. The sea's slightly mucky from the recent deluge but is altogether friendlier than last week, with far less weight behind it. We round the side and are walloped by waves refracting from the reef and the island.

We decide against going around, so play for a while then body surf back in. I wallow in the natural bubble bath where opposing surf collides over the sand neck, then trot up to the car park where Teri hands me a glass of mulled cider and Honey picks up a handsome black labrador and runs off to play ball with him and his family. Bubbly sea, wild weather, fabulous wild friends and a warming drink. A perfect afternoon.

SPITCHWICK
25 December

~

Driving over the hill with the low Christmas sun in front of us, we watch as illuminated swags of rain sweep down the Dart valley like angel hair on fairy lights. Honey and I squelch down the footpath from New Bridge, drowning in the roar of creamy flood water. At Spitchwick, the river is dark copper and slides like a serpent around the bend. I whip my clothes off and get straight in. The cold bites as I swim upstream, barely making any headway against the current. This is a day for sticking to the slower water by the near bank. As I dry off, we meet a Newfoundland-collie cross, who leaps in after sticks. A happy Saturnalia.

2013

HOPE COVE
1 January

~

I thought I was dreaming when opening the curtains this morning to be confronted with a bright sky and no rain! New Year, new weather? Honey and I drove in hope to Hope Cove. On the beach we changed to the wonderful retro sound of Esther's wind-up gramophone, its music swirling, slowing and quickening with the wind and laughter.

At Outer Hope a buffeted kestrel attempted to hover over the cliff. I'd decided against a wetsuit and was delighted to find that the rather frisky water, opaque with mashed weeds like toast crumbs in milky tea, actually felt warm as toast on my wind-whipped flesh. I dived in and was swaddled. A series of hilariously tortured faces followed us.

I struck out, ducking under the foam, swooping up over the rollers. JJ and Hugo had set off fast, so Sue and I waited for Esther and Claire. We swam round together and watched as waves disintegrated on pointy rocks. The Pop Art sky set off the lumpy water to form a gallery of stunning seascapes.

As we approached the beach we began to struggle with the breaking waves, the undertow and the hidden rocks. It was too murky to see what was coming; underwater, dark strips of weed flashed past.

I felt warm until I stood wobbling in the shallows, at which point the water ran from my body leaving it exposed to the nasty gale. After a shivering change I could still feel the chill radiate from my body as we wandered to the Hope and Anchor. When you're this frozen, layers of clothing act like a cool box.

Later, having warmed up beautifully, we walked the coast path to view JJ's latest plan: Round Burgh Island and on to Thurlestone through the arch in one swim. It doesn't look far from up there!

SIDMOUTH
6 January

~

It's a dank day and Honey and I drive through mizzle all the way to Sidmouth. As we approach Jacob's Ladder bright red cliffs burn through the hitherto relentless grey, and the pale sea appears to have been invaded by milk chocolate. Great drifts of pebbles like gulls' eggs clatter then emit an other-worldly shriek as brown waves break and snatch the water back leaving milky rivulets.

Bobbing along in the chill, I notice the headland between here and Ladram is trailing mist and resembles a speeding steam train heading out to sea.

Ducking under, I'm in an orangey world where I can barely see my own arms, the result of the pulverized chunks of cliff that have plummeted back into the sea after the wettest year in living memory.

BLACK ROCK
18 January

~

I trudge, head down, through the snow and howling easterly gale towards the river Lyd. Honey goes loopy doodle and leaves yeti-prints in the drifts. It starts to snow again, and I have to pull my hat down because the flakes are travelling so fast they feel like sand in my eyes. The view over Widgery Cross is breathtaking, and drifts blow to form knife-edged waves and ripples below the stone wall. Gorse flowers peek through puffs of snow like little suns.

I change under Black Rock, but it's not sheltered at all and the gale surges up the valley, riffling and rucking the surface of the pool. I was hoping to dip in just a swimsuit and boots, but the wind chill is seriously dangerous (I estimate it to be around -23 degrees) and Honey and I are alone, so I decide to wear a swimsuit, a rash vest, boots, gloves and a silicone hat. As I change, my legs turn cherry red, which doesn't usually happen until you've been in very cold water for a while.

I take a deep breath and brace myself for the freeze, smiling broadly. At the risk of sounding like Uri Geller, it really is all about positive mental attitude. Strangely, it feels warmer in than out and I don't get ice-cream limbs as I swim towards the falls. Light reflects from the snow, and the amber water glows like hot embers beneath me. I plunge under and become a firework as my skin burns and water bubbles explode from the cascade. I pop to the surface and float on my back, giggling.

I stay in for around three minutes, and although I'm tempted it would be foolish to swim some more. Slithering over icy rocks to leave the water, the wind slaps into me. I'm completely numb. I change rapidly, fumbling under my robe. My little cotton mat is frozen to the ground and I have to pull hard to unstick it. I dry Honey and we trek back the mile and a half to the car, by which time we're almost warm. There are no words to describe this exhilaration.

PRUSSIA COVE
16 February

~

A couple of posts from a weekend in deepest Cornwall. We descend the steep path to Prussia Cove, unsure which of the forks to take. One vanishes through a rabbit-hole in the shrubs. so we head that way like Alice in Wonderland. The sea glows Prussian blue between the rocky reefs.

It's icy cold, gently undulating and luminous in the shallows where patches of shell sand reflect sunlight. We can see each other's bodies beneath the surface even in the distance. We float back to the shingly shore through a narrow gap in the rocks which we name Aphrodite's Passage, in the spirit of romance engendered by such pulchritude.

PORTHCURNO
17 February

~

Gazing down over Porthcurno beach from the path by the Minack Theatre, I feel the urge to throw my arms wide and burst into an aria in celebration of its indescribable gorgeousness. It's a place where endless skies meet endless seas which slam into the cliffs and rebound in a seething mass. My hair is blowing horizontally, and my coat is luffing loudly. There are rips pulling the water back out to sea. Should I be sensible or obey the compulsion to leap into the ocean at once?

Far below in the car park, Matt has already decided to 'have a look', so the two of us change behind a slightly sheltered rock where my hair is merely at forty-five degrees. We watch closely for a bit and decide on an entry spot away from the area where most waves are crossing and where there is no rip. A couple of grey seals are surfing further out. Wading in, the undertow pulls the sand from beneath our feet and there's an unsettling sensation of movement while the landscape stays where it is and the sea churns.

I'm on my arse before the water's over my knees, and we're hit by wave after wave. Matt performs a star jump. As they rear up ready to break, the rollers are illuminated from behind like stained glass in the rarest pale turquoise. Legs aching as we fight the undertow, we're panting and laughing and diving through, over or under the breaks. We stay well within our depth; there's no way we can swim safely out. Finally, we body surf back in, landing inelegantly on the sand in an exhilarated heap. It's only then that I notice the cold.

VENFORD RESERVOIR
25 February
~

Our numerous attempts at Moon Gazey swims tend to be scuppered by the Devon weather. This evening, however, we were somewhat optimistic, this being the Imbolc moon that heralds the start of spring, the spawning of frogs and the lactation of ewes. The Met Office online map even showed a slither of moon peeking from behind a white, fluffy cloud at precisely the time of our swim.

And so it was that Honey and I stood in the car park near Venford in the dark. As our eyes adjusted, the pewter almost-glow of the water silhouetted the forestry evergreens that for some reason always clutter the shores of Dartmoor reservoirs – it's as though someone decides that if there's one man-made thing, no matter how beautiful, a few hundred thousand foreign trees sucking the life from the ground and upsetting the ecosystem won't hurt.

Sophie, Matt and Queenie arrived, and we toddled through the trees to the shore, where we changed in the frigid air and wondered what the water temperature might be. Sophie told us it had been just over one degree in the Dart on the previous day. A brief glow on the eastern horizon elicited a Moon Gazey frisson that swiftly morphed into the headlights from an approaching car.

In the end, the moon was provided by Queenie, who with her wild swimmer's twisted logic had decided that it would be less hassle to skinny-dip. Honey paddled, snorting softly, while the rest of us sidled in. The cold was almost indescribable, and we all struggled and howled. In the absence of the Moon Goddess there was nothing to distract us from the pain of icy werewolf talons of water shredding our thighs. I would honestly have got out had the others not been there to apply that all-important peer pressure.

We swam for a couple of minutes, chuntering, and then changed in the gloom before hurrying back to the cars. Half an hour later as we arrived home I still had frozen feet.

TINSIDE
25 February

~

A wonderful swim this morning in a sea that suddenly transformed to the colour and texture of mackerel skin as we headed out to the buoys. It felt cold, and no wonder – it's a mere 7.3 degrees, the coldest so far on Pauline's sea temperature graph. I had a proper cold water tan and got the biggest after-drop of the year having stayed in for longer than was perhaps sensible. Luckily, I was able to shiver my way down to Corinthians where I sat on the radiator and consumed a large cream tea.

SHARRAH
20 April
~

We've had several days of positively spring-like weather, and so we set off for Sharrah Pool, warmed intermittently by sunlight through the bare branches. Following the late freeze, there isn't so much an unfurling of leaves as a tentative peeking of leaf buds which continue to hug themselves just in case.

The Double Dart is not too full for the time of year and her depths are clear and amber, although there is still a suspiciously chilly-looking greenish-blue tinge around the rapids. We have two temperature takers who say 9 and 8 degrees, but it feels colder than that to my stunned body which attempts to shrink inside itself as I slide in. Several of us shriek. Honey cheats by wearing her fur coat.

I swim up and am more or less acclimatized by the upper cascade, where JJ forges across and clings to the far side. The water is gorgeously foaming and sparkling in the sunshine. I go in off an incredibly slippery rock and sail past in the rapid grinning and sinking as the energy fizzes through the needles of icy heat in my skin. I pass everyone else on the way up, faces dancing with light reflected from the choppy surface, hair ruffled by the cheeky gusts of wind funneling down the gorge.

Afterwards we scoff a trio of cakes: gin-soaked lemon drizzle, chocolate, and a colourful dried-fruit fest. I'm grateful for the warmth of my lovely Mammot hoody until Rachel, wrapped in a capacious white robe and carrying a lightsabre, tells me I resemble a sperm.

WEMBURY
2 May

~

Honey and I arrived at Wembury and paid an extortionate £4.50 for the privilege of parking before wandering down to join Teri and Michèle de la Mer who were staring intently at what appeared to be a nicely-coiled turd, but which turned out to be an adder; another had just vanished through a hole in the wall. The tardy arrival of spring had brought all of us out to bask in the sun.

We set up at the far end of the beach, about a hundred meters from the only other occupants, but were quickly approached by the National Trust man who threw us off for daring to have a dog with us. Apparently, there were some children due. I notice he didn't throw the polluting traffic out of the car park or close the lane in case any of them were run over, or spray Dettox around the rocks over which the sewage outfall discharges in wet weather. Bearing in mind I pick up Honey's mess, the sea temperature is still less than ten degrees, it's term time and mid-week, I can't see any problem at all with Honey being there. We pay huge water bills because of the cost of cleaning our beaches, and yet we're not allowed to use many of them with our dogs from May to October. I live in the country, I have a dog. I wouldn't subject her to a hot day in high summer, but why can't I go there at this time of year, or in the evenings? End of rant.

Anyway, we moved on up the coast path to a rocky gully where we sat and chatted and swam. I only managed about ten minutes, but it was so beautiful with the ripples focusing sunlight over smooth, quartz-striped pebbles and rocks. Entranced by the water swirling and lapping around the limpets on the rock where we got in, I was shivering by the time I got out. Apparently, limpets wander across the rocks in very slow motion and try to lever each other off. They reminded me of little Daleks.

BIGBURY-ON-SEA
2 May

~

Bigbury-on-Sea, Bank Holiday Monday: blue skies and wisps of cirrus, a bank of fog over the horizon, and the usual cheeky gale. It's low tide and light glints from the sand beneath the shallows and illuminates the sea so that it glows. We set up on the sand and chat while a few of our friends swim round Burgh Island, some for the first time. I'm hugely envious, but unable to join in owing to my shoulder injury.

We go to meet the first swimmers, but they take off up the stream towards the lifeguard hut like triathletes. Then we discover that the gang think they might have lost one of our newbies – but the lifeguards know exactly where he is, and sure enough he appears in the distance having become over-excited and taken the long route round the easterly reef.

Finally, it feels warm enough for a bob – and although I'm acclimatized, being unable to swim properly means the cold grips fast. We run in and I've no pain at all for the first time in ages. The actual water temperature is around 10 to 11 degrees, practically boiling point by recent standards. I mess around and play with Honey. Tiny waves break and splinter the light around us. It's like being on a cloud. Afterwards we continue to blether, wrapped in the smoke from barbecues and washed by the hubbub of people at play.

LONG TIMBER POOL
20 May

~

The water's cold – certainly no more than ten degrees. I slip in on the silted rocks and swim around till I feel warmer, staring up at the sky through abundant new leaves. Honey fossicks around Long Timber Tor – rather a grand name for what is a small conglomeration of rocks and gnarly old trees that barely rises above water level.

I climb out and change, transfixed by the little gardens of plants emerging from slender cracks in the rock. A warty, grey-green lichen covers the surface lending a Hammer Horror air.

Walking back, we're followed and bleated at by a hilariously horned and close-coated ewe who I'm guessing was bottle-fed, with an equally amusing lamb whose tiny pointed horns make him look like something from Narnia. Honey is utterly bemused.

THE LYD
29 May
~

I've just completed a run of busy shifts and am dog tired with a heavy cold. Several months' worth of Dartmoor winter fog has congealed around every cell in my head and chest. Honey and I head off to the Lyd for what I call my dose of Dartmoor Lemsip, but it's a struggle to walk down the track towards the clam into the wintry headwind. Usually a trotter, today I'm plodding at the pace of a townie handbag dog.

We reach the pool which is dung brown and strung with wads of vegetation along its edge where the rocks have sieved yesterday's flood water. I change and paddle in before leaping forward and under, surfacing between the twin stones that guard the falls like Modigliani heads. There's a hearty but bearable nip and I feel a mind-shift as the bubbles surge through and tug at my hair. The effect on my psyche is akin to stained false teeth plonked into Steradent, or an ancient penny crusted with grunge that emerges gleaming from a tumbler of cola.

Sun splays through the wind-whipped water and refracts from the river bottom in shades of gold and amber. I have gills.

MEL TOR
TO BEL POOL
2 June

~

A medley of pools today. Jackie, Allan, Honey and I are scrambling through bright sunshine and delayed-spring bluebells along the Poundsgate side of the Double Dart. The track is rather more suited to goats than humans and in places it's a mere foot-width across, hanging above the precipitous Dart Gorge by threads of roots, scree and loose soil. The bluebells are slightly faded, but their scent is still tangled with the roar of the river and the bright green leaves that oscillate and flicker the light so that I shiver.

We dip first below Mel Tor in one of the beautiful pools fed by falls that become part of the rapids in spates. There's a luteous tinge to the water and splodges of acid green leach from the trees. It's almost warm.

Wandering on, we stop of course at Sharrah, and plunge in from the rocks below the cascade. The northerly wind funnels down the gorge and ruffles the surface which shows its temperament of currents and eddies in a pointillist paisley of foam, like wrinkles on a face.

There's a mucky and slippery climb and descent over pink, polished rocks before we float into Lower Sharrah, a pool that's invisible from the Holne side of the river. It's a beautiful, fairyland place, heavily shaded by the high gorge on the far side. We step in to the puddle of light by the bank where the sun pours over the oaks above like a waterfall. A cave is secreted at the bend, trailing with ivy and protected from swimmers by the force of water from the cascade.

Finally, we stop at Bel Pool where Allan uses the rope and iron ladder to climb down from the track and leap in from the rocks. Jackie, Honey and I watch from the gods as he swims, diminished in size like an insect in amber. On our way back, we are mesmerised by a fluttering of butterflies and moths in brimstone, orange and blue, around bluebells and wood anemones. The May trees are finally beginning to bloom, a month or so late.

HORSESHOE FALLS
10 June
~

The water's soft and gorgeous, and that surreal, early summer-green light is tangible in the air around the pool above Horseshoe Falls. I dive in off the rocks, and the chill is warm enough to invigorate rather than shock. As I surface through amber in soft-focus it takes a few seconds for my ears to clear before the silence is replaced by the soothing sough of the falls. I swim upstream to warm up, then float down to the jacuzzi.

The pummelling and fizzing clears my mind and relaxes tired muscles after three long night shifts and four hours sleep. I'm wedged on a ledge that's softly clad in moss like a hairy chest; every so often I slide off and sink like a stone, giving myself up to the river while light sprays through bubbles and my skin tingles. I float again to the surface when the buoyancy returns below the falls, like drifting back to consciousness from a lovely dream.

MEAVY FALLS TO
NEWLEYCOMBE LAKE

14 June

~

I intended to dip by Leather Tor Bridge, an elderly and very narrow granite crossing of the Meavy above Burrator. There has never been a road here, only a hardcore track. It's a beautiful, gentle valley where the rocks and trees are softened by mosses and ferns, and where potato caves, their walls luminous with troglodyte lichens, hide beneath banks and rocks. The local farmers were evicted in 1917 to allow for a purer catchment and the eventual deepening of Burrator reservoir. Then the Forestry Commission littered this productive valley area of tiny newtakes, Devon banks, and fungus-clad beeches and oaks, with fast-growing non-native pines. Somehow in places the indigenous lushness breaks through the Forestry, like green satin knickers from beneath a witch's black cloak.

Honey and I climb over a stile downstream and pick and tunnel our way through the undergrowth and trees to a long and darkly mysterious pool. I find it littered with hidden black rocks and mostly not deep enough to swim in. I navigate and propel myself upstream with my arms to the little waterfall and lie back to let the river pass over me. The sound in this bongo-shaped haven is deep and resonant, and we're cocooned by trees.

We scrabble out and walk down to Newleycombe Lake (in this part of Devon, a 'lake' is a stream). Here in the lower clearing wild yellow flag irises are coming into flower. Wending down the narrow falls, I perch on a comfortably mossy rock and listen to the bubbling tinkles, plinks and plops of the water as it worms around roots and rocks. Hemlock sprouts everywhere.

In Memoriam (Part 1)
JONATHAN JOYCE
22 June

~

I don't want to write about JJ with a sad heart. He was pure joy; effervescent as a Double Dart cascade or a stormy sea; wild and wonderful and kind and clever and affectionate, and always up for anything. He was my friend and I adored him, a universal sentiment among our ever-expanding group of wild swimmers.

This is a series of fleeting impressions from an Atlantic Ocean of memories. Thinking of JJ, I hear his laughter echoing from the walls of a sea cave, I feel zings of adrenaline and the whoosh of a wave as we career through a sea arch having egged each other on, I see a blurred, ghostly form in a tiny tent as he shivers after an hour in Crazywell Pool during his acclimatization for a Channel relay. I see him bobbing and photographing shags and cormorants around the back of Thatcher Rock. I see his silly, yak-chewed hat and crazy jacuzzi hair, corkscrewing and tipped with mini-dreads from constant immersion in wild water. I see the sun shining and glinting off the sea as he smiles.

He was warmth in wind-whipped winter water and amber depths in a moorland river. He was a 'sinker' – a muscled and super-fit type who couldn't bear to carry the extra couple of kilos of blubber he needed in order for his legs to float; he was an amazing swimmer who flew through wild water like an eel with a jet engine. How we laughed at his expensive buoyancy shorts that added extra buns and quads onto his already legendary body. He took it all with good grace.

Walking alongside me on dry land, chatting as we climbed back up a cliff, or along the track through Holne Woods, JJ was quietly-spoken and thoughtful, or playful and funny, or challenging, and always interesting. He'd move among the group, spending time with everyone, head bent forward in concentration, discussing advanced swim training methods, or telling a funny story, or explaining an idea for a swim, or this week's twist to his famous gin-soaked lemon drizzle cake recipe.

Standing next to him in my swimsuit at Burgh Island as he pulled his wetsuit on (the one with the gold sleeves that he so loved), I once laughingly called JJ a wimp. He hesitated. Queenie piped up from behind with, 'She's got bigger balls than you have!'. He removed the suit and swam in trunks. He once signed up for an extreme endurance swim after I joked to him that he ought to be able to do it since he had a whole 5 days to recover from the 10k he was entered for; I should have known he'd have to go for it.

I haven't swum since JJ died one endless week ago, and when I do, I know I'll glimpse him just over the next wave, camera dangling from his belt, attempting to smile through frozen lips. He'll shoot past like a meteorite in Sharrah Pool, and I'll hear his voice in the cascade.

BUGLE HOLE
& MOTHECOMBE
23 June

~

Bugle Hole in early evening on a high spring tide and with a sporting swell is simply awesome. It looks like nothing as you meander down the cliff path, but once you're in you're swept along, hugged in the bosom of the sea, and pushed, squeezed, pulled and splatted against rocks if you fail to pay attention, as I did.

Waves crash and foam, rocks grow taller and shrink like Alice in Wonderland, and the blowhole at the end gurgles like a giant with IBS, despite being gobstopped by a buoy. Well worth the giant bruises.

Afterwards, we amble back to Mothecombe and collect driftwood for a fire. Then we lay out our lavish picnic and await the great event; the rising of the full supermoon above the headland. Allan and Kate's boys do a grand job with the fire, which has been carefully constructed by Rachel. We eat and chat and laugh, and Baa, Lou, Helen, Linda and Michele construct a moon from pebbles and driftwood on the sand as a kind of incantation, while slate clouds mass behind the beach.

Suddenly, she's here. Rising orange and dribbling a wandering reflection across the damp left by the receding tide on the sand, glowing and pregnant with our emotions. We toast our full supermoon and our dear, lost friend JJ with sparkling rosé wine. Then we change into wet kit and run into the sea, where Michele and Helen do cartwheels and we all body surf and dive and play in the breakers in the moonlight. The black clouds roll over, but JJ's moon forces cracks of light, incandescent through the darkness.

SALTER'S POOL
6 July
~

Four of us meet on the Double Dart for a morning swim in bright sunshine. Most of the pools in this steep-sided wooded valley are in shadow at this time of day, although the sun is creeping over the far bank and beginning to illuminate the water. It's beautifully cool and we finish our swim with a wild jacuzzi in Horseshoe Falls. The water is low, but there's plenty of bubble action to spritz our spirits to bursting point and I have a proper massage under the flume. We climb out onto the flat rock and warm our chilled bodies in a patch of sunlight before swimming back across to our rock, which is now crawling with happy teenagers out to enjoy this magical place on a golden day.

WALKHAM
8 July
~

It's baking today; Honey and I are hot and bothered. We set off for Grenofen at about 5:30pm and walk downstream towards Double Waters. We stop at the long, slim pool about halfway down. It's sheltered by beeches and oaks, in a place where the water is forced, tinkling, through a narrow channel. The rocks down which we step echo the course of the river with whorls and curlicues eroded by spates. I float through midges like electrons whizzing around the surface and feel the prickly, sticky sweat wash away. Where the sun dapples through the leaves the riverbed gleams gold and amber and resembles heaped coins to my un-goggled eyes. A dragonfly swoops overhead.

NEW BRIDGE
9 July
~

A quick early evening dip with Honey and Rachel; we go to one of the little pools just above the bridge today. The water is wonderfully refreshing and filled with fish – trout we think. There are two small jacuzzis here – one is hard to reach with the force of water, but I manage to stay in for a good minute by clambering over submerged mossy rocks then standing on one horizontally with my head and body upstream in the fizzing bit. The other is narrower with much less water coming through, and there's a handy curved nook in which to wedge. We wallow and watch the bubbles burst like Tinkerbells. I feel the tickle of the water and the amplified echoes of the falls in my underwater ears. Rachel says it's like bathing in champagne.

DARTMEET
13 July

~

The heatwave continues, and Honey and I are heading downstream from Dartmeet today in order to veg out on a rock somewhere and get very wet as often as we possibly can. There is a smattering of people around, most of them in the river. When we jump into the first pool, a couple who hadn't planned to swim join us fully-clothed to escape the thirty-degree, heat.

I don't know this upper stretch of the Double Dart that well, and there are endless shallow but swimmable pools on open moorland, then a sudden change of character as the river begins to rush downhill. In this lower part there are deeper, smaller pools, little canyons and waterfalls. The familiar ancient woodland hangs overhead; trees grow through rocks, roots thrust down to the water. A holly bush some ten feet above the river is draped with dried grasses – little flags reminding us of the potential power of this summery and benign-looking valley.

We wander, swim, float, shoot down narrows and sit under cascades. In between we lie around on hot rocks. Most of these are flat slabs surrounded by river and it feels like floating as the water rushes past at eye level. I read, do a bit of writing in my little notebook, eat my carrot hummus and pitta bread, take photos. Honey rootles around in the undergrowth or indulges with great focus and concentration in one of her absolutely favourite pastimes: bubble-watching. It's not often that I stop and just hang out somewhere, and the solitude is exactly what I need.

Beautiful desmoiselles are everywhere, and a bright orange butterfly plays around us for a while. I notice the layers of sounds that make up what at first appears to be the white noise of the Dart: soughing, plinking, deep hollow plops, tinkles, gurgles and then wave-like sounds that ebb and flow. We wander back up towards the car park when my skin begins to glow from the sun. I'm pretty tanned, but I have parts that are less well-acclimatized than others to an actual, full-on summer with sun and everything.

We arrive back at Dartmeet some six hours after we set off; I scoff a wonderfully cold strawberry cornet while Honey crashes soggily on her van bed.

SHARRAH
18 July
~

Baking hot, heavy air that's hard to inhale. Horseflies, midges. Salty, sticky skin. Laura and I slide into cool, rippling water and sink under gorgeous jacuzzi bubbles. After some time in Salter's Pool and Horseshoe Falls we steam up the track through the woods where even the boggiest patches are solidifying like overcooked chocolate brownies. It's cooler as we climb into the shelter of the ancient woodland, and the usual breeze funnels up the Sharrah glade.

You can't see the cascade current below the big rock, and the water in most of the pool is apparently flowing up hill in a series of slow eddies speckled with foam. We are able to swim straight up and into the falls, wedging in and feeling the full force without being snapped in two. It's usually impossible to get this close. Muscles loosen; atomised water mists our view.

When we get chilled, we prostrate ourselves on the flat rock on the far side and allow the heat to radiate through our bodies, moving

117

periodically to a warmer patch. Dragonflies and damselflies swoop among the whizzing midges above the surface, a series of deaths marked by plops. Small striped fish float silver and grey above bronze shadows in yellow ochre water.

We slither back down the silty slab and glide back upstream; a naked man swims past and we converse casually about the best pools and how to get to them. He gets out and is replaced by another, younger one who ignores us. Leaves rustle louder than the river.

SHARRAH
24 July
~

Today Kari and I have a special guest from the Big Smoke; none other than Mr Aquatic Ape (blogger of repute, Tooting Bec Lido ice swimmer, aficionado of post-swim cakes, and endurance sea swimmer). Kari knows AA of old, but we've never met in person before. We talk rather a lot on the way to Sharrah, then enjoy a lovely swimming and photography extravaganza in the golden water; the normally camera-shy Kari needs photos of herself in various aquatic environments for an interview she's giving.

I adore swimming with Kari, who treats swimming as an art form, but there are disadvantages because her artistic focus and unique coaching skills have previously resulted in some near-death experiences. ('You don't have to breathe' she says. Or: 'I'm planning to swallow dive off that huge rock into the sea as a performance art piece. It's only thirty-seven feet. Who's coming to high diving lessons?'). So, she wrestles the camera from AA and we are forced to spend some minutes underwater while Kari photographs us. In my case she wants to capture the shadowy zebra stripes on my body from the surface ripples.

Then I have to dive in several times until Kari gives up and AA manages to capture the event in chronophotography.

Later, Kari and I chat on the rocks while AA swims some more and Kari notices his left foot still kicks at an angle some ten years after she taught him to swim properly...

He escapes with a talking to.

BURGH ISLAND
24 July
~

Just before Christmas, Hugo and I had a rather large scare in the stormy seas off Burgh Island. A week later, I wimped out of attempting another circumnavigation in perfectly swimmable if rather large seas. Since then, when Burgh comes up I've been otherwise engaged, or it's been cancelled. Then JJ, a safe, super-fit and adventurous wing man on some of our more exciting swims, died in the sea, close to the shore, while on an otherwise unremarkable swim; a considerable chunk of my derring-do immediately vanished beneath the waves. In consequence, the whole Burgh thing has become a bit of a bogeyman for me. Aquatic Ape picked this up after our extended chat yesterday and suggested we should swim around Burgh this morning on the middle of the ebb tide.

It's a stunning and breezy day of sunshine and a bit of a Burgh swell from the south west. As we set off, the sea warms and we clear the easterly reef safely. I feel strangely distant and misty and almost short of breath as my body expresses the previously subconscious psychological whirlpool in my head. I had only met AA virtually before yesterday, on account of our blogging relationship. But wild swimmers somehow become instantaneous friends and I could not have wished for a better companion. He's a faster and fitter swimmer than I am, and he stops and waits for me now and again, chats, takes a few photos, and is just there, without being too close. He says if either of us were to get into trouble there's not a lot the other could do in any case!

We reach the entrance to what AA calmly calls 'the channel' which we locals more dramatically refer to as 'Death Valley'. It's quite churny, and I begin to feel the old Burgh magic as we forge through, adjusting for the direction of the swell, lost buoyancy and rocks. Then we are specks below the cliffs, sheltered from the waves and swimming in slow motion above and below the surface, seeing red and pink and green weeds wave in the submarine breeze.

We stop as we leave the channel, where the reef is scattered with pointed rocks. These appear and partly obscure as the waves crash into them. I try to suggest we should swim out and away from the rocks, but AA is having none of it, so through the reef we go. I feel short of breath and internally shaky again but am soon swimming with full concentration and watching ahead and beneath for the skin graters, until we are spat out into the swell. We bob for a bit, then work our way back in. I feel amazing.

MELDON POND
24 July

~

As we swim up Meldon Pond the rain hits; torrential, hammering Dartmoor rain accompanied by a rumble of thunder. We consider getting out, but we don't see any lightning and it's mesmerising watching the different types of rain hitting the water; its texture and colour morphs and melds into a misted band of spray over the surface of the pond. The water darkens and deepens in hue from turquoise to forest green. The raindrops grow in size and leap on stalks of water from the surface, before dropping back and disappearing into floating hemispherical bubbles. Smaller drops scatter pearls across the meniscus.

Afterwards, we walk back through the rain wearing our swimming gear and draped in soaked towels to Red-a-ven Brook which is close to spate. There we dip and play in a small pool where dark brown water forges and foams creamy and cool below the falls. The bubbly centre is like whisky and soda.

WESTWARD HO!
25 July
~

Westward Ho! is the only place in Britain that features an exclamation mark as a part of its name. This makes it sound vital and pioneering, as though overrun with pirates and pilgrims and maybe a cowboy or two. I spent most of my childhood in North Devon, and despite coming from a family who went out exploring at every opportunity, I don't remember ever coming here. So today I decided to have a quick swim in the lovely Atlantic after a shift at Bideford.

I followed signs to the seafront and parked for 85p next to a cafe and amusement arcade. Paying the fee necessitated entering the cafe, which was constructed entirely from plastic and overrun by people scoffing piles of anaemic chips, fried eggs, sausages the colour of exposed skin, beans, and bowls of what looked like diarrhoea, but which turned out to be 'curry sauce'. I left with the uncomfortable feeling that the perspiration on my brow had been impregnated with chip fat.

Clambering along the shingle bank was a relief; I stripped fast and tottered into the sea at high tide. It was warm and bouncy and deeply greeny-blue, with a nice thermocline in which my toes dangled from time to time as I bobbed. The smell of fried crap lined my nostrils like the scent of death, even when I looked out to sea. Next time I'll swim at Northam.

HINDU CAVES
18 August

~

This is one of Sophie's legendary swims, and she has persuaded us to meet at 6am in time for the sunrise. Honey and I drive across the moors in the dark, through torrential rain and swirling fog, before the rain slows to drizzle as we enter Torquay. Clouds are dispersing to reveal watery blue skies and a glow over the headland to the east. We change on the flat rocks and creep into the sea over savagely barnacled slabs, as the salmon-pink sunrise drips orange over the surface ripples and intensifies the red of the cliffs.

The caves are magical, chuntering with departing wavelets and studded with ancient shells and shingle. The sea transmutes through a disco-light show of colours from navy to royal blue to aquamarine, tinted with pinks and oranges and silvery highlights. Snakelocks stroke our legs.

Afterwards, we make a huge fry-up on portable stoves and chatter away. A young gull keens and pesters his mother for food. The sea siren calls us back for another dip.

STAVERTON BRIDGE
TO TOTNES
25 August

~

Today we're swimming the wider, lower, Wind in the Willows parts of the Dart between Staverton Bridge and Totnes. This is

Sophie's idea, and although I've driven along here many times, I've never swum it. At three miles, it is shorter than the other swim I had contemplated, and also populated with some nice dawdlers and a good downhill current which will suit my level of post-injury unfitness perfectly – or so I think.

We swim and scramble down through a languorous landscape where even the rapids are wide. From time to time I find myself spinning and being swept sideways across the rocky bottom. We slide down the weir – head first in Esther's case – then continue chatting and floating and fish-watching. There are some bright stones on the riverbed, which turn out to be coloured on their tops only with a kind of verdigris (algae, perhaps?).

The water by the banks is sieved through the roots of oaks and willows. Parts of the swim are eerily quiet as the river flows lazy and tinkle-less around wide bends. We float on our backs to watch as we hear the steam train passing with a wonderful hiss and chuff and a nostalgic scent of Victorian England. Sophie is almost asleep at one point, and I have to prod her as she swoops, eyes closed and head first, towards the bank at about five knots. I miss the gnome garden but catch a glimpse as we look back.

Eventually, Sophie, Lucien and I near the end and, being shattered, decide to climb out and walk the last couple of hundred meters. The lower reaches of the loop were not as fast-flowing as we'd expected, and so we have done a fair amount of proper swimming. My jaw is juddering with cold as we walk up to find the others.

We decamp to the White Hart Bar at Dartington and order an expensive dinner of tiny food. There is mackerel (around an eighth of a fish) with some foam and some beetroot and some venison with what appears to be goat's milk aerosol cream (this being Dartington). Being completely ravenous after a three-hour swim, we're forced to have cheesecake for pudding, mainly because we've seen some going out to a neighbouring table and it was visible to the naked eye.

DARTMEET
26 August

~

Honey and I went to Dartmeet this afternoon, and only just squeezed TrannyVan into the packed car park. We wandered downstream, but I could have counted the people we met on my fingers and toes. Our first dip was in the big pool only a few hundred metres from the bridge and there was neither sight nor sound of anyone. The water was golden and glassy, with every rock and fish and granule of sand clearly visible through the rippled reflected sun. The water today is noticeably chillier than of late and I felt a slight but definite skin burn. We dried off on the bank in the light breeze and warmish sun before trundling down to a faster stretch for a race up against the current. Squadrons of dragonflies droned around the bank.

WEST OKEMENT
30 August

~

This adventure was planned after I glimpsed wild water while walking the track above the cleave last week. Then I had sandalled feet and couldn't safely descend over the clitter to the river. So today some wild swimming friends have joined me for a sporting wild swim and waterfall exploration, in which we intend to walk up the river and into the cleave. This is not as simple as it might sound, and we soon find ourselves scrambling under and around stunted oaks, hawthorns and rowans on sometimes near-sheer banks, crawling on all fours and bouldering around monolithic, mossed boulders. About a third of the way we are forced to stop and change into swim gear and wetsuit boots, before dumping our rucksacks. From there we work our way uphill, mostly in the river.

We plop into a small pool. The West Okement's source is underground springs in a mire not too far from here and so it's chilly and peaty. We sit under the falls where ice-cream head hits fast and discover a variation on the wild jacuzzi; a wild bidet where water is forced upwards in a small basin between three rocks. Boswell, Stef's young labrador, is battling to deal with this new environment and attempts several giant leaps across pools. Honey leads the way, being used to such adventures.

As we ascend through greeny-bronze light, the falls become increasingly secretive and other-worldly; the Okement has found a way around and across and under this jumble of rocks and trees in the most picturesque way. The covering of black lichen like flaked burned paint and the soft layer of dark green moss allows us to get this far; wet rocks are like ice to grip.

We swim up a little pool where hunks of granite loom overhead. I feel like a microscopic lifeform. Allan photographs us as we sit behind the waterfall at the top end, inhaling the earthy smell and muffled sounds of dripping, velvety moss behind the shower curtain of water.

Afterwards, we climb to the track above the cleave and sit looking down. There is the merest hint of a ribbon of white water visible through the trees.

DEWERSTONE WOODS
4 September

~

Teri, the dogs and I climb the stone track through Dewerstone Woods above the Plym. This is the place where the river hurtles down the valley from the moors towards Plymouth and the sea. It's nippy, green-gold and shimmering beneath the cold, grey slab of the Dewerstone which looms above us in stark contrast. It's easy to imagine the horrifying legends associated with this rock, even in the late summer sun. 'Old Dewer' is the Dartmoor name for the Devil, and he has been known to drive lost travellers over the edge with his Whisht Hounds, headless dogs who live in Wistman's Wood. Any lost souls would land right on top of us in this lovely little pool where we are wallowing. A couple of climbers wave to us; they have ropes, luckily.

We slide and dawdle, float and chat, listen to the birds and the gentle tinkle and rush of the water. Honey has found a tennis ball and amuses herself by dropping it in the river and retrieving it; Devon, Teri's Jack Russell, follows us, hopping from rock to rock in deep concern for our welfare.

We arrive at the big slide and shoot off the edge into the pool; then we struggle to the cascade on the side. Teri goes right in and gets ice-cream head. Devon is stuck; she is lured into sliding down the rock, small wings of water behind each foot like a doggy Hermes. She plops into the pool and swims flat out to the edge before Old Dewer can steal her soul.

EAST OKEMENT

8 September

~

Another river scramble on Dartmoor; this time it's the East Okement, which cleaves the rock from Belstone Ridge through Halstock Woods. We have a nice little gang of explorers and, as usual when Deb visits from Kernow, 'things' happen. Today we walk a couple of miles to the ancient Chapel Ford, where there is also a clam bridge and steps, and descend back to the flatter area below the falls in order to change into our water gear. At this point, we are passed by an elderly and clearly vulnerable man, who stumbles and falls. He turns out to be missing from his home. Once we've escorted him back, slowly, to the waiting police and returned to our swim spot a good hour has passed.

We're now wet from the rain, and desperate to join Lucien in the river. The fun and beautiful part of the East Okement is a long, narrow sequence of cascades overhung by indigenous deciduous woodland. The rock is black and slithery, rippled and ridged in a negative of the river. Each little basin and gully is filled and emptied at either end by waterfalls. We don't dare to slide down the biggie which is around twenty feet high, ending in a flat rock rather than a pool, although we lean over and marvel at its dramatic curved turns. We follow Lucien and climb in from below for a pummelling.

Each pool lurks beneath near vertical walls and trees, and echoes with the sound of water gurgling and falling. Our breath mists the surface against the dark, dank rock and we're soon chilled and shivering. Such elemental beauty overcomes any discomfort, although as Sophie says, we ought really have done this during the heatwave.

LONDON BRIDGE
15 September
~

It's the day after the Dart 10k and some of our 'foreign' visitors have come to join us on a swim to London Bridge arch in Torquay. It's a bit friskier than forecast as stormy weather approaches, but the sea is still warm and the waves are not too big. Our first shock comes from the appearance of a conger eel on the beach – dead, luckily, as these big boys can have your leg off by all accounts; well, by the accounts of fishermen anyway.

I hang back with Plum and her daughter Poppet, who at seven is an amazingly confident and strong swimmer, dealing happily with regular submersion during her extreme bobbing session. They return to shore after a few hundred metres, and I catch up with the others near the arch. There are a couple of boys swimming with another visitor and they also do a fine job of taking on the stormy seas. I persuade a swimmer from London to keep going – he's more than capable but unused to these conditions. It's a good demonstration of the value of experience.

You can still see the cave entrance, but it's certainly too high and bouncy to risk going through. The water's so wonderful today, pointy witch's hat waves, turquoise and clear. The barnacled limestone sets off the colour beautifully.

The back entrance to the cave is largely sheltered since the swell is approaching more or less at ninety degrees to the arch. I venture in, but the gyre is filled with flotsam and jetsam which includes the usual plastic bottles and some unidentifiable stuff so I quickly venture out again, but not before marvelling in the deep petrol blue glow of the sea inside.

WEMBURY
19 September

~

There's a full moon due and predictably, it's a drizzly horrid day. But the cloud begins to lift at evening and the horizon comes into view as the sun drops. A brief glimpse of the plump full moon, gleaming pale gold. At Wembury, she remains hidden by the hills. There's a four-foot swell rolling gently to shore while the Mewstone lurks like a shark beyond the bay.

The sun sets without too much fuss over Wembury Point while moon-glow silhouettes the hills behind us, creeping higher and higher in a teasing burlesque till we are finally able to gaze on the full moon from the sea and swim across her spotlit path. Waves curve silver and shatter like mirrors.

BURGH ISLAND
19 September

~

Sunset, high tide, pretty flat. We set off and split into a fast group and dawdlers. The sea is beautiful, warm and welcoming. As we approach Death Valley from a clockwise direction we're assailed by crazy rebounding seas which always fascinate me; water somehow peaks and points and twirls here, mirroring the portcullis of dark rocks pointing skywards.

Queenie has swum across from Bantham and decides to go through the maelstrom reef on the final bend. Helen, Baa and I follow, but after a few minutes of foaming, sucking, rising, falling, dumping and churning I wimp out and turn back. Still missing a bit of my derring do...

Nonetheless, it's exhilarating. As we swim round to meet Queenie, the cliffs and our faces glow orange; we're pushed up by the swell in petrol blue metallic seas and the sunset is smelted through the tips of the waves in a stunning deep red splurge, before forming briefly into a molten ball on the horizon.

TOTNES
TO SHARPHAM
6 October

~

Honey and I stay at Bantham overnight but still manage to be late for our Dart swim (the first part of the Dart 10k route), thanks to the inhabitants of the Bantham Ham warren who lead Honey crazily astray. After Kari becomes uncharacteristically officer-like, we manage to get the correct number of vehicles (although without some of the kit) to the end of the swim at Sharpham before heading back to the start at Long Marsh in Totnes. We're only around fifteen minutes late starting for this tide-dependent swim, which is shockingly efficient by our usual standards.

This is the first time I've worn my wetsuit since December, and I'm mighty glad of it when I try dunking my face into the chill flood waters. It's early morning and the low, autumn sun and cold river are alchemical, conjuring a rare beauty of the kind that inspired the Romantic poets. Sun glints in soft-focus from lissome water while reeds and trees gather mistily on the banks. Rowers glide past almost silent, while V-formations of geese honk overhead.

The river is opaquely brown yet tastes fresh and clean. As we approach a marsh inlet I hear the tinkle of water draining; there are whorls where wrecked bladderwrack spins and I feel the whoosh of the tide pulling seawards. There's a slight whiff of earth and salt water. Even as we reach the Sharpham vineyards the river is barely brackish and knee-depth. Invisible creatures move upstream, their progress marked by trails of bubbles. We wade, sucked by estuarine mud, to the bank.

SAUNTON
10 October
~

I'm working in Bideford again today, so I meet Andrew for a dimpsey Atlantic swim at Saunton. The air temperature has plummeted and there's a frigid northerly blowing. The tide's around two thirds out, so we change in the shelter of the cliffs and trot down through the exposed widescreen beach. The first shallows are icy, but as we get to knee height the water warms so that it's infinitely preferable to go under.

The sea is dark, the same shade of slate as the puffs of cloud overhead. I'm lulled by the whoosh and foam of gently breaking surf as I float. The bank of cloud on the horizon obscures the setting sun from view, while the sky glows peach and palest blue and a crescent moon hangs tipsily over the estuary. Orange light shivers on the surface, distorted by long rollers and the latticed ripples formed by the wind as it whips offshore.

We stay in slightly too long, bobbing, swimming and bodysurfing. As we run back up the beach my feet begin to freeze, and by the time we reach the car park I'm numb to the ankles and able to sprint straight over the stony ground with no hobbling whatsoever. Well perhaps 'sprint' is too strong a word. We warm up in TrannyVan with ginger tea and a chat.

SPITCHWICK

15 October

~

Rachel, Honey and I meet for a late afternoon dip at Spitchwick, and are pleased to see another, bikini-clad wild swimmer whom we don't know. We do know that the water has chilled, but nothing can prepare us for the shock of the winter-level temperature today. The autumn twigs and leaves are piled high on the riverbed, and you might think the soft duvet underfoot would help with the cold; you'd be wrong. It's like lying naked on the steel floor of a commercial deep-freeze. Poor Rachel slips on a hidden rock and goes straight under, inhaling the chilled water and coughing for several minutes. Eventually we are able to pootle with staccato strokes through dark water in which golden leaves are suspended. Low sun adds dreamy magic.

SHILLEY POOL

9 November

~

Honey and I accompany Matt and Aaron on an exploratory trip to Shilley Pool. We wade and scramble poolward over sodden ground dotted with clitter and clumps of rusted bracken. Matt drops knee deep into a bog. Blackaton Brook is a tiny tributary of the Upper Teign and looks like nothingness with the colours of the open moorland leeched by mizzle and the rumbling water secreted beneath dark undergrowth.

Suddenly all is revealed; a series of smooth rocks curve gently down into the near-circular pool which is dammed by boulders at the lower end. It starts to rain heavily as we arrive, and we slide in from the top to slow-boiling water. It's like swimming in a mixture of Guinness, Jail Ale and ice in a pub's drip tray at the end of a busy night. The infinity pool effect looking downstream is gorgeous. We reckon the river temperature to be around 6 to 7 degrees, chillier still than the Teign where we swam earlier. It's strange how your brain interprets this level of cold: the burn of my body could be from heat, while my hands feel a painful freeze.

SHARRAH
17 November
~

Holne woods aflame today and bespattered in a pointillist celebration of hot colours. Aish Tor rises like an over-proved loaf behind Wellsfoot, rusted with autumn bracken. The water, meanwhile, is chilling rapidly. Today it looks almost black.

Sharrah is icy and voluminous. We gasp and swim staccato to the rapids, which we descend in clouds of foam. Our newbie cold-water swimmers do well to get in at all. Eight degrees, but it somehow feels colder – perhaps that's the effect of fiery autumn woods raising our expectations. Anticipatory thermogenesis, one of JJ's pet theories, certainly came into play today.

TINSIDE
26 November
~

I hadn't been in the sea for a while, so when someone suggested a swim at Tinside this lunchtime I was there in a flash.

The sea has chilled rapidly and is now around 10 degrees, enough to give us full-on ice cream heads. There was barely a ripple in the water, and it had that metallic sheen which forms with a bit of cloud cover and a low winter sun on the horizon.

We chatted as we swam and discussed the psychology of the missing yellow buoys which used to form a kind of boundary; now there's no reason to stop swimming, nor to swim between points. Strangely liberating.

We changed and jigged around with afterdrop. Then we sat at the Terrace café with warm drinks and hotwater bottles, looking out towards the Breakwater. Below us a cormorant fished close to the beach, a shadowy streak under the gin-clear sea popping up to gobble her catch just a couple of feet from the shore.

Returning to the car, poor Rosie was caught like the hapless fish by two Great White traffic wardens: a parking ticket.

WEMBURY
10 December

~

Met the gals for a wonderfully wild swim at Wembury today. It was shortly after high tide, and the breakers were perfectly-sized; large enough for some proper fun but not so big as to cause us problems with getting back in, nor indeed for a repeat of Teri's 'stunned sea bass' impression. Wintery sun seeped through wispy clouds and forged the surface of the sea into molten aluminium.

The messy waves peaked in points, backlit as we leapt to beat the breaks like so many aquamarine stained glass windows. Chilly water, but nowhere near the freeze of the weekend. I felt a glow of cold radiate from my body, which lasted only briefly as water slapped and walloped us from above. We played and bobbed, marvelling in the light show while we chatted and laughed. Small rafts of seaweed swept past. There's nothing to beat a wild winter sea.

2014

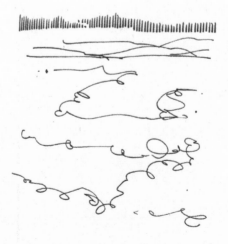

WEMBURY
2 January

~

Finally we managed to swim today after endless storms and flooding. I've been hammered by a cold and cough over Christmas and was desperately in need of some chilly, frisky water. So, off we went to good old Wembury where the forecast 7 to 11 foot surf wasn't too bad at low tide, and water and air temperatures were both conveniently ten degrees.

We frolicked in the surf, bobbed around and chatted. Low sun gave two totally contrasting views: one (out to sea) in shades of mercury; the other (towards shore) in technicolor. The seabed resembled a yarn shop at sale time with heaps of ankle-grabbing, tangled, ripped up weeds, and the water was khaki, opaque with pulverized sea life.

Afterwards, we loitered around Tony's fire, ate, drank Teri's mulled cider and shoved hot rocks from the windbreak up our jumpers. An effective way of warming up from the inside.

WADHAM
18 January

~

Wadham is a secret cove accessed via a precipitous track, and it's normally frequented by nudists. Rain tips and pours downhill and it's January, so we allow ourselves the luxury of layers of fleece, woolies, waterproofs and wellies. As we pick our way from the cliff top we notice there is a patch of light over the sea, and sure enough the deluge stops. By this time Honey, who has been groomed to within an inch of her life by my mother, has transformed from a beautifully fluffy cream puff to a mud-bespattered, drenched mop. Of course, she's found a tennis ball. We scramble the last bit –

which is more of a mountain-bike drop than a footpath – and spy Richard on the beach waiting for us. His family have refused to leave the car.

The rocks are Dartmouth slate according to Richard who's done some research. It is layered and striped in shades of bruise, and small bodies of it pop up from the shingle beach like the undulations of a Loch Ness monster. We change and plunge into bouncy water, which is stained with mud yet still maintains a blue-green tinge to the predominant battleship grey. It's not too cold and being engulfed feels like heaven. Michele and I pootle out towards the end of the reef where waves are waterfalling and sucking. In the end, I go fairly close and allow myself to be pulled rockward for a while.

I swim some of the return in backstroke and when I turn over I can see Jackie's customary flower bobbing up and down; a summery, bright pink splurge among the hundred shades of grey.

BLACK ROCK
31 January

~

The tempestuous weather continues unabated, and although I like it wild it's playing havoc with my swimming. There's wild, and there's wild. Today, Honey and I stomp through black peaty mud the texture of molten chocolate. We make squelching noises that resemble a liquidised meal being chomped by an octogenarian with badly-fitting false teeth. The pool at Black Rock thunders and the edge of the dam has been washed away. I strip and wade carefully in before plunging under and popping back up like an ice cube in a whisky and soda. I daren't swim across.

WHITSAND BAY
18 February

~

It's a real shock this – a sunny day! Sadly, our plans to swim at Tregantle are foiled thanks to Second World War beach defence ironmongery that's been uncovered by the recent weeks of extreme storms. So, Stef and I pootle down to the middle of the bay and descend the cliffs with the dogs. It's low tide and we're concerned about the recent doggy deaths from eating boulders of palm oil washed up on local beaches. Luckily there doesn't appear to be any here. Instead, there's a gingery heap of ripped kelp, alive with flies, and a hail of plastic scattered across the sands. Mist veils the rocky reefs and razor shells lie smashed like little car crashes, spilling pale sausage-shaped bodies the colour and texture of clotted cream. And there's the sound of the sea, soothing and enticing...

By the time we wade in, the sun is glaring at a winter angle. The water here pulls and swirls in several directions between the outcrops, and there is a diagonal wave and a nice big rip feeding out from the near reef. As I pop up from a wipeout I see white puffs of cloud on the horizon that echo the foaming white water perfectly. It's beautiful, exhilarating, invigorating. The waves dump from eight feet, silky walls of water that rise and curl suddenly before crashing down. Sometimes three or four catch up and we're in a sea of bubbles. Small fountains erupt from the surface like the ghostly fingers of wrecked sailors.

Afterwards we change slowly, soaked in the warmth of the winter sun; or perhaps the heat is generated by the young couple canoodling in the cave entrance behind us...

SHARRAH
21 February

~

We haven't swum here for ages thanks to the storms and constant rain. There are exposed roots in Sharrah glade like nerves in a flailed body and the track resembles a dry riverbed.

The river is surging, and Elephant Rock barely raises its head above the surface.

Today is not a positive embrace-the-chill sort of day for me. We dawdle before taking the plunge and when we do it's like being savaged by a colony of frozen ants. We all struggle to get upstream and are pushed into the rocks. To the right is a gently curvaceous surge, which turns out to be more forceful still than the choppy stream by the bank. There is a mere smattering of natural foam; usually when the river rages we swim through a beery head at least a foot high.

By now, I've contorted into a frog pose and my stroke is more of a judder. By kicking off an underwater boulder and sprinting between the two currents, I make it to the rock. The rapid is spectacular, like the tangible roar of a polar bear. We sink a fair way down before popping up with the dissipating bubbles. The water is greenish as though tinted with absinthe and sets off our scarlet cold-water tans rather nicely. Six degrees of wonderful.

DARTMEET
27 March

~

We'd already decided to go for a Double Dart dip today, but peering from my bedroom window I see snow on them there Tors. Jackie, Allan and Helen have come from the southern side and haven't seen the snow, so we decide to drive back to Dartmeet to make the most of it. It's gone from the valley, but there's a good few inches at the top and the temperature is a mere two degrees, although the water is considerably warmer at – gulp – six. I'm not acclimatized to this and I know it's going to hurt.

Jackie floats almost serenely, but even she grimaces briefly from beneath the big flower in her hair. She says it's lovely, but I don't believe her. Helen and Allan begin swimming, and now it's my turn. It feels like hugging a slab of iceberg before having it ripped from my body inch by inch. I scream. Lots. Then I swim – ish – and stagger out. Honey thinks it's hilarious and goes loopy doodle on the bank with a full display of doggy guffawing. I try again, which usually works, but not today.

DARTMEET
1 April
~

A day of whipped wind, wispy clouds and watery blue skies. Honey is frisky; I feel heavy, chilled and tired. We walk from Dartmeet and I'm soon sweating through my t-shirt and summer fleece. Honey skits along, paddling and snuffling among the tree roots. It smells of spring.

We rootle around, picking our way through juicily-mossed tumbles of clitter and exploring sculptural stumps and dams left by the incredible winter spates. One dam is at least ten feet above the river level, a wicker wall of bleached, fractured tree limbs, wads of washed-out grass, twigs and bracken, curved like a river current. A speeding toad passes us then dives into a bed of crumpled oak leaves.

A couple are frying bacon on the flat rock from where I meant to swim. We go in further down, sinking through heaped sub-aqua sand dunes. The current pulls hard and swamps my grey mood with water the colour and sweetness of Sauternes. There's a perfect level of nip; it's far warmer than last week when I struggled to stay in.

I scramble out and walk up to the narrows, where there's an unexpected turquoise hue. It's an easy slide down the mossy rocks into the cascade where I swoosh, suspended in a cloud of bubbles, my knees and hip smarting where frozen skin connects with rock. The river rolls me to the eddy. Bumblebees buzz past followed by a low-flying Chinook, both sensed rather than heard, the difference between them mostly one of scale. I wade to the bank and my cold-water tan burns. We wander back upstream while the roar of the river swirls into birdsong.

THE ERME, BUGLE HOLE & MOTHECOMBE
14 April
~

Today we plan a three-pronged attack on Fiona's attempt to swim in 60 new locations in her 60th birthday year: The Erme estuary, Bugle Hole and Mothecombe beach – a triumvirate of Devon swims within a single meandering mile or so of each other. Since my back has given out, I leave the first swim to Fiona, Helen, Honey and Boswell while Stef and I natter on the beach. Luckily, Joe saves us from being cut off by the incoming tide which we'd rather embarrassingly failed to notice. A rapid swoosh up the river with the flood is one of the wonderful adventures described in Roger Deakin's Waterlog, and it's high on our list for the summer.

Around teatime, we return to the car park and load up with

food before wandering down to Mothecombe. Four of us amble along the coast path to Bugle Hole with the aim of hitting it at high tide. The sun has just departed, and it feels far colder than it is. Once in, I regain my mojo and allow myself to be coddled by the magnified Bugle swell. The last of the sun hits at the far end of the passage where we float in a sparkling wonderland of rocks and aquamarine sea. Honey joins us, but I have to help her back through the magic cauldron where we're gliding through the water one moment, stationary in the centre of the pool the next, and then flung into the barnacled cheese-grater rock to finish.

Back at Mothecombe, flames gutter through Alison's driftwood fire and we begin scoffing as the sun drops and colour leaches from sea and sky leaving a watery, diluted metal effect in shades of shell pink and wishy blue. Gradually people depart, leaving me, Fiona, Helen, Joe, Honey and the dogs on the beach. We wander across to the western end of the sands as the light granulates into darkness. There, above the headland, dangles a splendid full moon, its watery track melting across the sand and the receding wavelets.

Helen and I have decided not to go in again, while Fiona is keen. The Moon Goddess, of course, works her magic, so we strip for a skinny-dip. Although the sea is still nippy at between 10 and 11 degrees, it feels delicious; who could ask for more than the creep of sea on bare skin, a water-stroked body, the scent of salt, the whoosh of the waves and a shimmering magic pathway to the moon (we are studiously ignored by the two bonfire loads of teenagers swigging beer and toasting sausages on driftwood sticks.)

We clamber back up the track in moon light and moon shadow on numb feet to be greeted by a transcendental view as we reach the top of the headland. Below us the Erme and the ebb tide rush out to sea while waves run inland over the top. The summit of each breaker gleams silver, and the various eddies and wavelets where water fights over sand bars shoal into visions of fish. We stand transfixed at the curves, waves, ribbons, and the witch moon.

DEWERSTONE
18 April
~

I creak up the track towards the Dewerstone at slug-pace, dreaming of the calming effect of cold river water on my back injury. It's a gorgeous day of sunshine and glittering cascades. The pool refracts light the colour of new leaves, and the roar of the falls blitzes my ears as I doggy paddle. Teri and Jane slide down the pudding rock and clamber through the keyhole, while Honey plays her Dewerstone game of dropping her found tennis ball from the ledge fifteen feet above, before scrabbling down and swimming over to collect it from the eddy, over and over again. I bob to the falls while a grey wagtail bobs on a nearby rock. I clamber out refreshed and watch Teri floating her worries away.

THE TAVY
24 April
~

It's unusual to have guests on my side of the moors; for some weird reason I'm an isolated wild swimmer in wild swimming heaven, but today Helen is visiting from Exeter. We pick our way down from Hill Bridge to one of the closer pools. There's a precipitous pebble shelf half way up, a microcosm of the beaches at Beesands and Slapton. We stumble over goose-egg stones and drop in to the deep water, tasting the peat and the spring. It's twelve degrees, and the river has lost her winter tint. It feels right to float again in bronze. Because of my back injury, I've developed an upright doggy-paddle floating walk and can't get close to the cascade, but Helen swims in and wafts through bubbles. The branches hang bare above luscious, erupting banks.

BEL POOL
4 May

~

Rich green vegetation is ruffled by a cheeky breeze that gathers and flings birdsong in snatches. Brimstone butterflies, bluebells about to burst, wood anemones. Golden green light and a warm spring sun. Bel Pool looks still from the lower end, cuddled by trees in new leaf. My bare feet slither on silted rocks in the shallows, and I cling to the debarked fallen tree that's been there ages. I can't imagine how it's survived the huge winter spates. When I swim, the water's far colder than expected – 10 at most. The little rapids at the top rush into sight and hearing together, just where the black, dripping crack in the side of the gorge sneaks into my peripheral vision. Here, spring is sucked from the air and I can almost see trolls sidling out. Honey puffs to the island and boings off after a scent. My skin is flushed with cold and burning as I dry off.

WONWELL
5 May

~

I'm never at my best in the morning, and today I've only had a couple of hours kip in the TrannyVan after a housewarming party. It's five thirty. Wonwell is a small, isolated beach at the mouth of the river Erme, more or less opposite Mothecombe. The tide's out and it's almost light as we walk down and dump our stuff. There's a delay before anyone gets changed; I always feel cold when tired, and there's a chilly wind. Finally, we trot down to the sea which feels considerably warmer than the air, and wade in through long, low waves that break on the sandbar as the tide begins to flood. I can't swim fast because of my back, and I'm really noticing the lack of exercise-generated heat.

There's a grey-green-blue coolness to the water, then it starts to transform as the sun peeps over the hill. I'm floating with Honey maybe a hundred yards out, and there's a moment when a warmth begins to suffuse me that must be purely psychological. A peachy tinge ripples then dissolves through the surface and the water beneath becomes bluer. I swim back to shore with Honey who is swamped by a couple of waves. By the time we return to the rocks I'm shivering, and the sea is a good hundred yards closer than it was when we arrived. Joh's crutch, meanwhile, has been swallowed by the incoming tide, and will no doubt intrigue the person who finds it washed up one day.

We set up our camping stoves and cook tomatoes, eggs, bacon and eggy bread for breakfast. I'm ravenous. Steph, being German, eats a sacrilegious combination of crumpets fried in olive oil with jam. Carole has made bacon and egg cup-cakes, including some with veggie bacon for me. We light a fire, then warm and smoke ourselves. I give Honey her ball, which somehow ends up in the fire. Luckily someone notices and kicks the ball out shortly after Honey has attempted to extricate it with her paws. Then I see her lying on the beach breathing smoke like a dragon; she's holding the hot ball in her mouth. I grab it and cool it in the stream, but she doesn't seem to have suffered at all.

This was the inaugural swim of our new wild swimming group Into the Fish Dimension, which has an artistic and environmental ethos.

146

THE LYD
25 May
~

Continued downpours have left our little river the colour of Jail Ale and with a foaming head. Helen and I were intending to skinny-dip, only there's a couple just downstream setting up camp for the night and a lone walker on the far bank heading our way. So, we wimp out and don our cozzies.

We duck, swim to the waterfall and explore for a time till I notice Helen is mid-strip. I join her, and we toss our swimsuits over to the rocks. Although we're almost naked, Helen is wearing goggles and I a pair of neoprene boots. How very English. So we whip those off too and lob them to the shallows. The surge beneath the big rock resembles ghostly frogspawn and I imagine ranks of frogs squatting in the depths, bums aloft.

We take turns to swim breaststroke against the flow. So many sensations and far more subtle than a jacuzzi: cold currents that push and pummel; effervescence like birds' wings brushing on skin, fizzing louder than the roar of the cascade. Each bubble oscillates and atomises on our faces. Our eyes are level with the surface, so we see tiny spheres meld and grow before scatting across the pool in the wind. There's nothing to beat skinny-dipping in this exposed place.

BEL POOL
25 May
~

It's a beautiful morning, and we can still smell bluebells although they're past their best. The Dart is middling-high after the rain, and the colour of a pub ceiling before the smoking ban. As we change at the lower end of Bel Pool a foam berg floats past, revolving gently in the current. It's fairly easy to swim upstream on the island side, then suddenly I'm whipped by a speeding eddy to the cascade. Floating backwards, the cappuccino foam splats spurts and spumes in a crazy dance, sending us over to the rocks. I climb up and leap in; it's invigorating to say the least. The sun hasn't quite reached the pool, but I feel the warmth as I contemplate the fresh oak leaves overhead. The juddering afterdrop shows the water is as cold as it felt.

BLACK TOR
4 June

~

Today's dip stems from a sudden whim to visit the little dell below Black Tor where we haven't been for some time. I have no towel or swimsuit so it's a skinny-dip, clinging to mossed rocks like hairy pectorals in the surge below the falls, in a howling gale, just before the storm hits.

Afterwards, I stand spreadeagled on the bank while the wind whirls and chills still more. Flicking the drops of water from my skin with both hands, I turn and slowly dry. As I dress, slinky grey stripes of rain advance from Burrator. Water runs from my hair and down my face, and my sandalled feet are frozen from squelching through sucking boggy tussocks. Honey has the wind up her tail, so cavorts like an excited camel, then eats some perfectly-matured vintage horse poo which means a choice between warming my soaking feet with the van heater and fainting with the pong, or winding the window down and breathing fresh, cold, Dartmoor air. You can guess which option I choose.

HARTLAND QUAY
7 June

~

The plan today was to swim from Hope Cove to Thurlestone, only with a pesky southerly blowing we thought it might be a tad frisky. We went instead to Hartland Quay where we found the usual crashing and foaming around the rocks; it's almost always wild around here.

Andrew, Plum and I got in fairly easily off the sheltered slipway and began to bounce in glowing, aquamarine sea. Earlier we'd been on the more reckless side of a Facebook debate on the dangers of being struck by lightning while swimming, so of course we were interrupted by a crashing rumble that I initially took to be a big wave dumping on pebbles; obviously it was thunder. We laughed in its face and continued with our swim, reasoning that there are plenty of high rocks and cliffs around here to attract strikes and we're barely breaking the surface. Anyway, nothing short of death was going to get us out of this slightly nippy lushness.

The geology here always takes my breath away. Reefs like crashed wafer biscuits point out to sea, overwhelmed by cliffs layered and snapped into jagged points like petrified storm waves. We swam over and back to the big rock from where Andrew climbed and jumped while Plum and I bobbed, pulled this way and that by the crazy currents from waves surging through and around rocks.

After around three quarters of an hour we walked back up the slipway and sniggered at the potential irony of being struck by lightning before we got to the pub but survived to order a pint of Tribute each. Inside, in a dark corner, slouched a young couple watching movies on an iPad. Two hours later they were still there, Skyping their friends about the lovely weather. Really.

In Memoriam (Part 2)
JONATHAN JOYCE
16 June

~

One short year ago yesterday, on 15th June 2013, Jonathan 'JJ' Joyce died suddenly. He was loved by many, and he created the Outdoor Swimming Society Wild Swim Map which exemplifies his nature of exploration, discovery and sharing.

In common with many of JJ's swimming friends, I find he pops into my mind while I'm immersed in wild water. This weekend of sun and watery fun was one he'd have adored, and so he spent a lot of time in my head. We swam and later skinny-dipped under the full Honey Moon at Bantham wearing floral headdresses, swooshed up and down the Aune Estuary with the speeding tide, and dipped in a pool and waterfall in the river Tavy on the high moor. JJ's spirit was there, enjoying the thrills, the social banter and chat, the different types of water and cake, and the unusual cloud formations on Friday at dusk which would have intrigued him. We mentioned him, and memories trickled into conversations.

In the two short years that we knew him, JJ (and his family) became so much a part of our swimming and social lives that the hole resulting from his shocking death appeared like a disused mineshaft, swallowing large chunks of our world with it. Yet he gave so much and touched so many of us in different ways, that his presence remains tangible.

He transformed people and was instrumental in developing some of our favourite swims and our ideas of what is swimmable (just). I wouldn't have done a few of the crazy things we did without him there. He reinforced the notion that it's perfectly normal to run into the sea at dawn wearing 1920s fancy dress, and discovered that gin improves lemon drizzle cake no end.

WATCOMBE BEACH
TO BELL ROCK
13 July

~

Few diary entries this season: it's partly due a smorgasbord of injuries that appear to be roaming from joint to joint like a hen night. Anyway, I had my pesky shoulder injury injected with hydrocortisone almost two weeks ago, and since we're supposed to be taking on the beast that is the Gulf of Corryvreckan in August, I thought I'd better give the shoulder a try out.

So off we went to Watcombe Beach. I lived in Watcombe from age three to seven and have many happy memories of the beach and steep walk down to it, but I haven't been there since...1968. It's a gorgeous little cove surrounded by red sandstone cliffs and woodland. The end chunk of cliff sports a considerable crack down half its length, so it won't be long till that tumbles down into the sea.

We swam out stroked by kelp on a low spring, in sea that was misted and coloured shades of aquamarine. Constellations of starfish were scattered across sandy patches, and once we reached the caves they multiplied to a veritable milky way. As ever on this piece of coastline, the colours of rocks and sea zing in a perfect Matisse palette. Although the sea was flat calm, it sucked and soughed through the cave, cooler than outside and stinking of seal breath. Layers of life-forms meshed on the rocks to form a collage of mineral, plant and animal, so that it's hard to see the divide between life and death.

I swam across to Bell Rock but felt too cold to sidle through the slim gap. I also suspect after months of limited exercise that my capacious arse might have caused me to wedge fast in the narrows where I would probably stay till the next low tide. So, Nancy and

I headed back, leaving the rest to forage and exclaim. I managed I think around 300m of front crawl, with little in the way of pain. Here's hoping...

BANTHAM
10 December
~

A full Cold Moon draws us to Bantham, where we meet to swim in the Aune ria. We build a bonfire and use it to light home-made torches. There is an arterial sound and energy here, of lifeblood whooshing upstream on the flood tide. The scents of salt and woodsmoke meld, and we trail flames as we wade in.

Frigid water glows in orange ripples, while above glares a phosphorus moon escaped from the glove of a passing cloud. Sparks shoot in the steely edge of the sea wind and hair flies like the flame from my torch. Warm thoughts and wind-burned cheeks tussle with chilled bodies. On the far bank, from a glass-walled house, silhouetted figures watch. We form a circle, shadowing the moon who has lured us and the sea to her.

2015

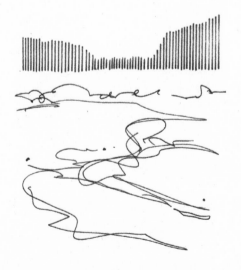

MOTHECOMBE
7 March

~

A last-minute call to dip at Mothecombe, and boy is it worth the trip. It's mid-flood and surfy, the spectacular estuarine break is at its peak, and a strong, chilly wind cuts through our prematurely spring-like clothing. Rachel, Linda, Honey and I make our way to the shelter of the disused tidal pool. Honey thunders off after a tall, dark and handsome retriever while the three of us change.

The rip drags at our legs as we teeter in, shivering, so we cross closer to the surfers and into the teeth of the wind. The water is muted turquoise and made icy by the wind chill. We contort into dance shapes to stay dry as we wade deeper; wild swimming oxymoronic behaviour if ever I saw it. Linda is resplendent in her Dahab souk hooded neoprene singlet, while Rachel is wearing a mini ra-ra skirt and a purple flowered hat. As I float between Egyptian Ninja and Devon Cream Tea Lady, a large wave breaks over my head, dousing the Dali dreamscape.

SHARRAH
& BLACK ROCK
8 March

~

Sharrah today is middling in flow, fairly nippy. As the clouds clear it's bright and sunny, but still rain falls as if from space. Our new swimmer Lorna, friend of a friend, shows us all up by diving straight in off the pointy rock wearing only a swimsuit, gloves and boots. It takes me a good two minutes to get above the waist.

We stop at Elephant Rock for the kayakers to descend, a great view from close up, and chat to the two alongside while we wait.

Then it's a quick swoosh down the cascade, ice-cream neck, and out. Ten minutes is plenty as this is only my second skin swim of the year.

As ever, Honey manages to crash bodily into both Jackie's and Helen's biscuits, scoffing several with the speed and lack of finesse of an American eating competition winner.

On the walk back, we divert to Black Rock where Lorna, Allan and Helen leap into bubbles and play around again. Allan strips half way and does a skinny circuit of the falls, bottom glowing like the moon through white foam, before slinking out.

EAST OKEMENT
& TAW MARSH
22 March

~

A gorgeous but cold day, taking in a few hot swimming spots. We start in the East Okement, being wholly unable to resist the top waterfalls. Clear water and sunspots the colour of barley sugar. The water's very, very cold. The dogs are ecstatic, bounding between river, rock and leaf mould, panting, steaming and snuffling.

Someone finds an eviscerated tawny owl, which Rachel slings in a bin liner for later examination. It swings sadly in its makeshift body bag beneath her rucksack as she walks up the cleave towards Nine Maidens. There we play around with some gorse stump foraged by Kari which resembles labia, rather appropriately for the stone circle that is most probably a paean to a moon goddess, perhaps Artemis or Hecate.

There's a rather surreal twenty-first century army ambush occurring in the middle of the track where we're heading, so we're asked, very politely, to wander elsewhere. As we cross below Belstone Ridge all hell breaks loose, except there's more smoke from Alex's e-cigarette than from the grenade below.

Taw Marsh is stunning in the spring sunshine, weeds wafting green beneath the surface. We're all thinking of the pre-Raphaelite Ophelia, and Kari decides to recreate Millais' version with Linda and some bracken. Linda lies supine in the water playing dead, which at that temperature is no mean feat. As Rachel pushes her off and leaps out of the way for the picture, Lily and Fudge photobomb before the hair floats downstream. Less Lizzie Siddall, more Dartmoor Moses.

As we leave, we realise we've left behind Philippa, Linda's historian friend. We call her with whistles, and she returns, thrilled at the discovery of some black and glittery rock that she's sure is a type of tin ore called cassiterite. This reminds me, as Anna has just pointed out, why it's fun to walk and swim with such variegated people who together form a human encyclopedia.

WELCOMBE MOUTH
28 March

~

Honey and I are in North Devon today on a work-related visit and take the opportunity to return to one of our favourite beaches. Welcome Mouth is a part of that wonderful area of cliff on the North Devon/Cornwall border where the earth's crust has been pushed and snapped into points that rise up to 400 feet above the Atlantic. The Atlantic breakers have crashed into these cliffs over millennia to erode fingers of rock that cleave the sand at 45 degrees and claw out to sea.

Drifts of pebbles form waves around the cliffs which resemble smooth soft grey gulls' eggs ringed with quartz.

It's almost low tide, and there's a fair swell and a drizzle that might be spray from the waves crashing along the reefs. The sea is opaque with a tint of Rich Tea biscuit. We trot up the narrow sandy tongue to be splatted almost at once by excitable foaming water, marbled, crashing and sucking. It's not too cold. I'm tempted to head beyond the break, but the backwash is hideously strong and I'm afraid that Honey, who's nearby, will get caught and pulled into the break zone. Crazy diagonal waves jaywalk back out, so I don't spend long with my feet off the ground.

A dog walker tells me she swims from May to October, and that the sand is only recently returning after the huge storms of 14 months ago, grouting the gaps between reef fingers.

2016

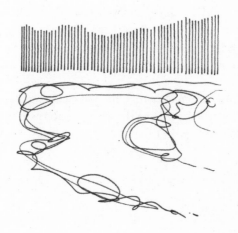

EDITOR'S NOTE

The last entry in Lynne Roper's swim diaries was made on 28 March 2015. The following passages are taken from a separate journal – Out of My Brains – that she began in early 2016 just before diagnosis of the brain tumour that would end her life in August that same year.

Some of her most powerful writing can be found in this second collection, still available to read online. Passionate concern for the NHS, a paramedic's attention to her condition and its treatments, attempts to find meaning and purpose as she approached end of life: Lynne takes us to these hard places in the same way she shared her wild swims – in language that is rich, vivid, unsparing. Life-affirming.

While I have selected here only passages where wild waters continue to feature, I believe the wider concerns of her writing at this time can be heard in them too.

BURGH ISLAND
20 February

~

A text from my friend Plum, who's suggesting she comes down for the weekend and we go somewhere nice. Yes please.

Plum:	Out of interest, how do you feel about dressing for dinner?
Me:	Dressing for dinner? I have no clothes, I've grown out of all my dresses...
Plum:	Well, I was thinking of the Burgh Island Hotel and I've always wanted to stay there so you've given me a bloody good excuse.
Me:	Seriously?!

She calls back a bit later – not only has she managed to get us in for one night on Saturday, we're also booked into the Mermaid Suite, which overlooks the famous Mermaid Pool, built by damming an inlet on the side of the island so that it remains filled with sea water.

Being wild swimmers who regularly frequent this area, we've naturally visited and enjoyed this private pool on a number of occasions. The difference is, we've only ever been before in a slightly less than official capacity. The normal raid involves swimming round the back of Burgh, going covertly up the gully to the dam, before scaling the rocks and sneaking in. I think we might have to skinny-dip just to make our official swim less legit.

I'm so excited! Texts Plum. So am I. Once there, we're picked up by our Slovakian driver and over we go. I think of the Simpson's episode where Homer joins the Masons. Another world of luxury is revealed: different entrances, different approaches.

A glass of chilled sherry, bags carried up, and there's a bottle of Sauvignon Blanc on ice from Kari in the sitting room of our suite.

We start with a postprandial sauna, then wander sweatily to Reception for our green outdoor towels.

'You're going swimming? I've been already today!' The receptionist laughs in a strong Eastern European accent, arms waving and eyes rolling. (Many of the ice swimmers on the various outdoor swimming social media channels are Eastern European, the kind who cut a hole through ice with a chainsaw and pay a man to row around all night, so it doesn't freeze over before the morning dip.)

We sneak into the pool, as spray splats over the little dam and across the surface. I don't feel confident in my balance or movement but am able to swim a little, puffing, while Plum heads across to the wilder side. It's blooming cold, 6 or 7 degrees we reckon.

The seas here are spectacular and often huge, and it is swimmable on the right tide at times when you'd think getting in was certain death. That's why this is one of my favourite swims. Now though I'm looking out from the aquamarine stillness of the pool at the wild sea where I'd more usually be found. I remember once glimpsing the pool from the top of a huge wave while playing the lookout game; you swim gradually closer to the rocks then allow yourself to be lifted heavenwards on an approaching wave as it towers and rears in preparation for crashing down into the rocks, suspended momentarily on the top of the world. It's a life-enhancing experience to look over that precipice and drop off the back before the final crash. But for now, I'm cocooned with the mermaid.

BURGH ISLAND
21 February
~

An utterly marvellous weekend at the Burgh Island Hotel with Plum. We chat about all sorts – wild swimming, the rise of lidos, cancer and metastasis. We eat beautiful meals and drink Mermaids' Kisses looking over the raging reefs towards Bantham.

I tell Plum my big fear: *Losing my mind.*

The possibility of dying sooner rather than later, of there being no point in worrying any longer about developing those chronic conditions of later life with which I am so professionally familiar – this isn't foremost, although I have considered it in a slightly detached way.

I don't want to lose my mind.

We sleep with the windows open, washed in ozone and the myriad sounds of the sea. If you're by water, stop, close your eyes, and just listen for as long as you can. There is no single sound, no permanently dominant noise but rather a soundscape map that you can follow with your ears as the water moves. Beneath the roar here, there are distant wafts of gentler soughing, tickles and tinkles, the champagne fizz of dissipating foam, a sudden boom as a wave crashes onto the reef and echoes around the Mermaid Pool cove.

What's the origin of those crashing sounds? It's air bubbles that form in rough water and which act as little bells, oscillating in suspension till they pop. Such a beautiful image, bells in the sea.

Plum's also arranged a Sunday dip at Burgh (as if there were any more ways in which a friend could be wonderful). Around twenty of our wild swimming crew arrive, and I'm able to tell those who don't already know about the tumour and then watch as they frolic in the rough seas. I'd love to go in, but if I get knocked over I don't have the confidence to know I'll be able to recover. Best not take the risk today.

We retire to the Pickwick Inn for lunch. I show a picture of the MRI scan to various people, and somehow the tumour gets named Hunt, after our less-than-esteemed Secretary of State for Health.

'Bugger Off Hunt!' I shout. There's a period of hilarity as everyone joins in.

'Where is he in your head? Turn around, turn around I can't see him!'. Jackie – kind and gently glamorous mermaid, wearer of flowers in her hair – is giving Hunt the nastiest evil eye I've ever seen. 'Hunt – out!'

This lunch, and the naming of Hunt with my dear swimmy friends, is where it all crashes past me like a flood tide up the River Aune. *Why me? What for? What do I do?*

What I do is write. I'll tell it like it is. If I do get good news, then brilliant. But it's the now I mustn't lose. I'll write about our excellent NHS, which is here for me in one of the most difficult and tumultuous weeks of my life; the same NHS I worked for over the past ten years.

What scares me most?
Losing my mind
Losing our NHS

BANTHAM

1 March

~

I'm thinking mostly about my hospital bed situation and still haven't heard from neurosurgery. Today we go to Bantham for the first day of filming the wild swimming advert, and without this day to look forward to I'd have been in a spin.

It's a complete diversion, during which we film a piece in the Sloop Inn where we discuss cholesterol, before heading outside and shooting two swims and a good deal of cavorting (I'm not very good at that at the moment). The brief for the ad involved swimmers aged over 50, and so a key question we're asked to discuss during the filming is age: how we feel about it, how we exercise. We are all active, though the majority are certainly not athletes. Attitudes to aging and illness interest me greatly, and I did have a pang about today because I'm not working – I really can't – yet I spent a long day yesterday doing what I could manage. I wasn't sure I'd do the swims but am so glad I did. Overhanging it all is the thought of time: *How much do I have left? Do I wait to die? Will Hunt be able to grow over the weekend to the point where it's too late for it to matter that I have no bed and therefore no op?*

The crew, led by Becka the Director, is fabulously funny, professional, and friendly with that kind of boundless energy that suffuses all. They run backwards over the sand with cameras. We also get a lovely lunch at the Sloop. I have fish pie, thinking again of brain food. It had struck me as I chopped nuts for muesli earlier that the things I eat to ward off dementia (bogeyman) might well be helping Hunt, since he's likely to have mutated from those same brain cells.

I struggle with the first river swim, because it's at the time of day (late morning and early afternoon) when I feel worst, related I think to the steroids. The water is cold too, and I can't really swim enough to warm up. I have no core left, it wobbles in a most odd way. I was left holding a GoPro while Dave and Kari showed off their butterfly.

The sea part at the end involved walking into the white horses and a screaming gale while our legs were sandblasted. I managed to stay upright, while earlier I could barely balance to pull my boots on. I'm invigorated and exfoliated, but when I check in hope the abrasion has been sufficient to thin out my leg hair I find them to be as woolly as ever. I daren't shave because manual dexterity is a bit of an issue, as is balance.

I wonder as the late afternoon sun splinters and glares off the sea whether this is my last opportunity to get in it, certainly for some time; I find myself consciously storing the memories, forming that image in my mind and holding it there like a lantern. The light, the crazy currents and foam, the Avalon view of Burgh suspended in spray, those sea bells, the scent and fizz of ozone as I breathe.

WALKHAM
3 March
~

My face feels squashed somehow. I wake to find I'm prodding some padding beneath my cheekbones and have ditched the pillow. In the mirror is a harvest moon, where once was my face.

Ten years younger, lines plumped out. People pay a fortune to look like this. I peer into the speckled glass: *Mirror, Mirror, on the wall, whose is the fairest face of all?*

I prod and note the bulges beneath my eyes and the pads filling what was once the gap between cheekbones and jaw. Ah, the jaw. There's a chin there, but on either side hang rococo swags. The whole is coloured in a spectacularly healthy-looking windburn shade of the type sported by mountaineers striding over crags. No fading Victorian maid for me then, no romantic drape of wan helplessness across a velvet chaise longue (Mum actually has one of these which I had been planning to put to good use later on).

J and A arrive; "Don't you look well!" Bloody steroids.

We head off for a walk down the Walkham, me wobbling slightly but feeling quite good. Honey fossicks in the woodland and swims with J & A in a gorgeous, green-tinged river pool. This one features a chalybeate spring, where iron colours the otherwise palest blue-grey rocks to a dramatic rusty red. I examine the spring, and the tumorous galls on a sapling rooted next to it, feeling a connection. I'd love to leap into those lush bubbles, but the chill of winter river temperatures (perhaps between 5 and 7 degrees) is hard to counter when you can't forge through in a strong and warming way.

MINOR INJURIES UNIT, TAVISTOCK
19 March

~

One of our favourite wild swims is down the river Aune from Aveton Gifford to Bantham. We go on the high spring from towards the top of the tidal reach, and swim down three and a bit miles with the ebb. The top stretch is silted mud, and the water opaque, greeny-orange and brackish. When you swim here you disturb the silt, releasing bubbles from dwellers in river mud. I know there's a world under that brown gloop, a deeper, chthonian world I'm brushing with my hands as I pass. Lower down, as the salt water sinks beneath the less dense and cooler river, there's an area where methane from rotting vegetation is trapped beneath sand layered lightly by currents. As you tread, you feel your feet are on clouds and streams of bubbles rise as you move, tickling your legs as you sink back into the water.

My head contains now a mix of those sensations, and perhaps some Dartmoor mire; it's like one of the places I used to take my nephews bog-trotting, where you run and the ground wibbles and undulates as you pass.

It started with a need to blow my nose. I did so gently and was surprised by bubbles blipping up from the left nostril beyond my eye. Air in the sinuses. Then when I touched the top of my dressing, the bog in my head began to bubble and squish. Reading the information on craniotomy, the piece of skull is replaced with screws, but is prone to lifting and moving till the bone heals and I guess that's what I'm feeling, along with the swelling from the op.

The brain and spinal cord are encased by meninges or membranes, which have beautiful names: the dura mater is the tough mother, the outer protection; the arachnoid mater (spidered with blood vessels) sits beneath; and then the pia mater is the soft mother, the membrane covering the brain itself. Between the latter two is the subarachnoid space, filled with cerebrospinal fluid (CSF) that acts as a protective buffer. Those membranes have been cut, and I hope restored. Something I'll ask about later: how do they repair such fine entities? To notice fluid moving from within is most strange.

CASTLE DROGO
15 April

~

Our wild swimming group made its first patchwork blankets for Jackie when she got married, and then for Linda when she became seriously ill. We decide on a broad colour scheme and square size, and individuals either crochet, knit, felt or appliqué squares and add-ons which they post or bring to a bee for stitching together. Yesterday, a few of us met at Castle Drogo to see the Grayson Perry and Louis XIV tapestries currently on display there, and I was given the fabulous blankets made for me by my fish friends afterwards.

I once saw a fairly prosaic mainstream film called How to Make An American Quilt that resonated despite its shortcomings. I hadn't previously considered heirloom quilts or the stories they carried. In this film, the quilt is stitched as a wedding gift for the heroine by her grandmother, aunt and their friends, to a theme. Our patchwork blankets continue the collaborative, individual and social traditions of such crafts.

My beautiful blankets, and the muffler and bag, represent a map of friendships forged through a common love of water and nature. It's about shared adventures, shared confidences, shared scares, shared perspectives. Some of those who made and sent squares are wild swimmers I'd only 'met' online.

There are all kinds of styles, interpretations, and approaches to both crafts and the world stitched in, with flashes of inspiration and unique embellishments abounding. I love them. It's overwhelming to receive such a gift. My mum was completely overcome when I showed her and spent ages looking at each element.

Kari's square came attached to a piece of ribbon; she made it from sterling silver and copper. It features the MRI scan of my brain tumour, replete with cerebral oedema. How Grayson is that?

I give thanks from the bottom of my heart to all who crafted my blanket. A cuddly map of minds, friendships and aquatic adventures.

SHARRAH
13 June

~

I made the Sharrah Stagger three weeks ago: a total of five miles up the Dart and back, culminating in a swim in the beautiful pool. The event was organised by a visiting friend who finds it very difficult to walk any distance, and it was one of her long-term goals to swim there; two other friends also have mobility and health problems, so we decided to stagger together. It was a Sunday and I'd had two days with no radiotherapy, though I'd taken the Temozolomide as usual. I'm pretty sure I wouldn't have made it on any other day.

We were accompanied by a few other friends on the opposite end of the fitness scale, who were delighted to join us. I had no real concern about safety because all of us are outdoors people and wild swimmers who take the perceived risk as a part of the point of doing it; we like a thrill, and we like to live on the edge. Nonetheless, I found myself feeling grateful that if anything were to go wrong we had someone able to scamper up the steep sides of the Dart Gorge to get help.

Things didn't quite go to plan.

We made it to Sharrah slowly but uneventfully, with a picnic lunch of carrot hummus, guacamole, pitta bread and gin lemon drizzle cake at Black Rock. I found myself eventually sitting on a rock with water up to my shoulders. The water was still pretty cold, maybe 10 or 11 degrees, and I was afraid of being unable to breathe properly. It's that core confidence that's missing, that certainty my body can respond, that I can swim like a fish and get myself out of trouble as I have so many times before. I have little faith now in my body doing anything beyond failing. The fit and athletic me hasn't been there for at least 18 months, and since last autumn I've lost it completely.

I remember meeting a friend at Polzeath just before I was diagnosed. I went out about 300 meters in a wavy but not strong sea and had a real surge of fear as I started to swim back that I couldn't make it on the ebb. I did, by taking it slowly and steadily. This time, I felt similarly. But shielded by J, I made it up to the cascade and sat on a rock.

There was a teenage couple there. The boy was wearing boxers and hesitating on the edge, while his girl was swimming happily in a bikini. We joined her in calling encouragement and he finally took the plunge.

I felt a surge of energy, watching two young people really going for it and having so much fun, so I decided to come down the cascade. Of course, I hit a rock and naughtily grazed a knee and one calf. I almost did the half dive to go under, but for once chose the sensible option and kept my head above water. In bubbles you sink because they make the water less dense. At the same time, the current pulls you along and so the feeling is like being blown by a gale through a puffy cloud. At Sharrah, there's a sheer rock face and the current pushes you into it, so I bent and kicked as I neared it, managing to partly cross the current and head downstream. I felt warm, buffeted and exhilarated as I got out.

'Could I have the Germolene?' said a voice to my right. I looked over and realised that J had fallen over, with C now holding a tissue over J's right shin. Being a paramedic I'm more inclined to the Germolene approach than a dial 999 one. However, as C lifted the tissues from J's shin I found myself coming as close to leaping into action as I have in months. J had fallen into a rock and lacerated her shin over the bone (known in the trade as a pre-tibial laceration). Beneath the laceration was clearly a varicose vein. Dark blood welled and poured.

I grabbed a wad of tissues, got the others to raise J's leg and to press hard on the wound with the tissues. People worry about arterial bleeds, but if you burst a varicose vein you can bleed out. I wasn't in a position to take J's blood pressure (if it's high, the bleed can be spectacular).

As I was travelling light, I'd made a decision not to carry my first aid kit, and so I had no dressings with me. I got the others to help J dry off and get dressed – she was both shocked and cold from her swim – and fished in my rucksack for tissues. Had a look at the wound and allowed it to bleed a little to clean it as best I could, then used my wodge of tissues taped down with micropore to maintain the pressure. Fortuitously, J was wearing knee-length pressure socks which meant we had a simple and effective way of maintaining the pressure evenly over the wound. After a rest and some more picnic, J was sure that she'd make the walk back.

Rather more exciting than we'd planned, but a lovely boost in several ways. Honey was also delighted to spend the afternoon in the woods and river, back to her old life.

AFTERWORD

SOUL SWIMS WILD
Editor's Afterword

It was May 2016 and I had just begun what would become a two-season feat of long-distance writing beside the country's oldest lido, Pells Pool in Lewes. As its writer-in-residence, I determined to write a mile on scrolls of pool-length paper. There are many true stories about what propelled me, one of which was a wish to recover for myself a sense of girlhood self-sovereignty – a straightforward belief and pleasure in my strength, skill and shape that adult life had diminished in me, as for so many women. I was following myself back to source, and arrived at my childhood beach in the West Country:

> At nine I was in love with myself in my body in a way I
> missed ever after and have had returned to me only now,
> past 40, through this pool, and my strange undertaking with
> its fairytale proportions. Back then, back there, I loved the
> soft fluff on my legs that went gold in the sun so I looked,
> to myself, spell-bound. Even my bruises and plasters pleased
> me: I counted them like coins; my treasure. Status symbols.
> I was brownest, the most hardy. And when we went each
> evening through summer to the freezing sea at Widemouth,
> just along the jagged black coast from Bude, I would throw
> myself against the waves, holding up my heavy home-made
> surfboard like a shield.

New online, with a website that had no followers, I posted these words to no one it felt. Instead, they called forth an immediate response from Lynne 'Rivers' Roper: the woman whose words I would spend months immersed in after her death.

There was no small talk. Her approach was frank and urgent.

She had read about me: we had a shared West Country upbringing. I had survived a sudden near-death experience a decade back, holding ever since a constant sense of extra life; she had recovered from breast cancer but was dying now of a brain tumour. I was a hospice life-story scribe; she was a paramedic: we didn't shy away from lives ending. I was calling for submissions to an anthology perfect for her work – *Watermarks: Writing by Lido Lovers & Wild Swimmers* – but she was too ill already to edit and send a selection. Would I find readers for her swim diaries after she was gone? And could we talk together about living wild in the face of death? I was, she assessed with the skill of a paramedic and wild swimmer both, a woman who could go the distance with her in this.

So we began. Emails exchanged until the last weeks when her words began to run together and eddy beyond my ability to decode them. This one from Lynne in June 2016, two months before she died, is exemplar of her courage and clarity:

I'm thinking so much about where I am in my life, and
its ending.

The treatment that's just finished was hard, and the effects
are still growing like an incoming breaker. I feel pinned to
the bottom after a wipeout: a bit of pummelling then, when
you just try to relax and stay beneath the turbulence, you
feel the weight of the water and don't know if you can get
back up in time to breathe.

I found wild swimming, met all these amazing people,
and things started to happen. Then the brain tumour started
to make itself known, just as I felt I was beginning to find
my purpose.

Where do I want to go with this? I want to make meaning.
I find meaning through water, and the relationships it
nurtures. So many women – especially of a certain age –
are drawn to water and to each other.

In the Tavy recently, I felt very weak physically and afraid;
my body no longer remembers what it should do, and my
brain's too slow. But I went under the water and swam
along about five feet below the surface with my eyes open
to water the colour of an old penny. When we'd finished,
I felt so renewed, like holy water.

That Lynne could write like this at end of life, after surgery and
strong drug treatments, was all I needed to make the promise
this book keeps: to publish her diaries so others can share in
her love of wild water and the rich connections that come when
people gather to swim in it.

I hope every copy of this book – now and in the future –
is read outdoors beside wild waters in the West Country and
beyond. May they go waterlogged, sun-buckled, wind-chapped.
And may readers share in the bliss Lynne discovered in these
elements: *'It's a spiritual experience, sliding through wild water.
Worries dissolve, my mind is liberated; thoughts flow and glide and
play like dolphins. My soul swims wild.'*

To souls that swim wild, then. In words and water both.

TANYA SHADRICK
Editor

RIPPLE EFFECT: LYNNE ROPER AT
THE OUTDOOR SWIMMING SOCIETY

You might not have known Lynne, but chances are a ripple she set off has touched your shores. During the years Lynne kept her diaries, she had another role alongside her work as a paramedic: a volunteer for the Outdoor Swimming Society.

In 2012, The Outdoor Swimming Society was six years old and Lynne answered a cry for more support. She had back problems and was facing the prospect of leaving full-time employment in the NHS. I had my own issues, holding myself and the OSS together with a terminally ill mum, a one year old and new pregnancy. I loved the fact we never talked about any of it. Our brief snatched phone calls went like this: "How are you?" – "Fine" – "How are you?" – 'Fine"; joint knowing laughter, and then straight into the work at hand.

The 'work' itself was ludicrous: no income attached and no clear need to be doing it. But we were both committed: passionate about swimming, we determined to share it with others. The outdoor swimming movement in the UK was still in its infancy, and we were among its biggest champions. We liked our swimming wild and free, full of joy and adventure, without tow floats or limits.

On that first phone call Lynne said she wasn't a writer (oh how she became one!), but she would 'try to help out'. Soon Lynne and I were the OSS hub, from which all communications generated. She fitted her swimming around her shift patterns, saying that water washed away the stresses of the job. But she also made room for a lot of voluntary work: OSS book reviews, newsletters and content; manning the warm-up tent at our events.

We were both far too busy to talk about our 'stuff', and so I never read Lynne's online diaries (how lovely to have them now in my preferred reading form). All I knew was that Lynne was fun and full of the best contradictions. She lived a frugal life on Dartmoor with her bonkers dog while embracing all the good things of the digital age. She wanted to teach people about safety, but she 'hated bloody tow floats'. "She was the best driver I've ever known," says Kari Furre, her friend and an OSS Director, but this was a skillset put to use in 'a hippy van'. To demonstrate her control "she drove at breathtaking speed but oh so smoothly so as not to bounce an imaginary casualty in the back," says Kari. "Even the dangling toys in the windscreen seemed to flow along."

We shared a lot, including the death of our friend and key OSS figure Jonathan Joyce in 2013. But it is the differences between people that makes the Outdoor Swimming Society interesting, and Lynne's contributions to the growth of a movement are indelible.

She was a woman with an impressive breadth of experience: her Arts degree meant she could understand 'art speak'; a military career left her unphased by patriarchal nonsense; paramedic training gave her medical knowledge and scientific understanding while also making her practical, fearless and empathetic. Lynne was also political and had many friends with similarly strong principles and special interests. Such a rich background meant she could communicate with most people in their own language; however, if she disagreed with anything she was able to argue her corner, not frightened to stand her ground.

She had so much charisma it travelled the waves of the internet, and she was a scrapper. The outdoor swimming community was growing and taking shape but rules of engagement were not yet written; while I cowered from combat, fearful of trolling, Lynne would get in there. Kari and I followed with joy the Facebook threads where Lynne was standing her ground. She was brave like that – and those acts of bravery shaped and protected the community as it grew; she kept the space safe.

Her online engagement meant in a very short time she 'knew' many people in the swimming world. As the numbers of outdoor swimmers increased, the interests of the community started to subdivide – ice-milers, skinny-dippers, wild swimmers, cake dippers, marathon swimmers, skin swimmers. Super-connectors like Lynne stopped us from getting diluted, keeping the community richer and more interesting, while growing it exponentially.

In her swimming she was fearless, loving to tackle rough seas, journeys around rocks, and skinny-dips at midnight in black, inky water. She rarely wore a wet suit, and was well-versed in the vagaries of rivers. She would also, if asked, take the hand of anyone who asked, helping them over their fears and into water. (During this period she founded two local swimming groups, Devon & Cornwall Wild Swimmers with Pauline Barker and, later, Into The Fish Dimension).

She was flamboyant and unapologetic, not hiding the scars of her double mastectomy – at one point she even had a Facebook page where she posted inspiration for mastectomy tattoos. ("Although she swam too much to ever put that plan into practice," says Kari. "You have to stay out of the water for some time if you have a tattoo.")

As press officer for the Outdoor Swimming Society, she developed safety advice and helped communicate with the media on the the joy of wild swimming and how to take educated risks.

181

She was not afraid to speak after a tragic death – her paramedic background made her confident to do this without upsetting the bereaved, and she knew it was important to swimmers' freedom to counteract misinformation. All of this was a gift from her to a cause and community she believed in.

In time, Lynne wrote one of the most important developments at the Outdoor Swimming Society – our website's 'Survive' section: a distillation of the collective emerging wisdom on how to understand water and swim outdoors safely (but without limits).

Before she grew ill, Lynne was making plans for a book, and a water safety course for swimmers (something completely new). She wanted to realise an experiential course that would help people understand the water they swam in, to take informed risks: a course that combined landscape, water and common sense.

Lynne died peacefully on Saturday 13th August, 2016, aged 55. She was buried at Sharpham Natural Burial Grounds, attended by friends, family and her OSS community. It was the day before the Dart10k, and her funeral wreath was taken there next day by friends and strapped around one of the photo frames that crown the glory of finishers. Around 1600 swimmers swam past her grave, and smiled underneath her funeral flowers, wearing bracelets bearing a scrap of poetry she and Kari had made into an art installation: *We find ourselves at sea.*

Kari (who appears often in this book) described to me recently Lynne's physical world: she was a woman with the brightest costumes, wildest hats, and floppiest harem pants, whose home contained cerise sofas, witches in crevices, and a staircase painted like a seascape. ("Naturally I was very rude about all the colour," Kari said, "but I wish I could ring her still from my side of the moor for an evening chat."). However you have pictured Lynne while reading this book, it is probably not like this – and this is one of the things she (and all of us at the OSS) love about being the water: it transcends normal boundaries, shares spirit and spreads commonalities rather than differences.

We miss Lynne in many ways, and are still trying to catch up with her vision. Enjoy her ripples.

KATE REW
The Outdoor Swimming Society

RISKS OF WILD SWIMMING

"There's a point at which wild swimming becomes dangerous, and as a swimmer who loves the exhilaration and challenge of wild water it's vital I understand where that point is."
– Burgh Island, 16 December 2012

Wild Woman Swimming documents Lynne Roper's passion and skill for swimming outdoors in locations she knew well. By swimming outdoors you are at heightened risk of serious injury and harm, including hypothermia, drowning, sickness and injury (for example from wildlife or underwater debris).

The decision to swim at any location described in *Wild Woman Swimming* must therefore be taken individually, and swimmers must not rely (in whole or in part) on views or information presented in this book, which is a journal not a guide.

If you are in any doubt about the safety of a swim or your ability to complete it, you should not enter the water.

A location that appears 'safe' for a strong outdoor swimmer can be perilous for a weak, insufficiently-acclimatised or non-swimmer. A location that has a good safety profile one day may be perilous the next as a result of (for example) heavy rain, or, conversely, drought and lower water levels.

The 'Survive' section of the Outdoor Swimming Society website provides further (but not comprehensive) information on risks and how to moderate them.

outdoorswimmingsociety.com/category/features/survive

INDEX OF PLACES

MAP

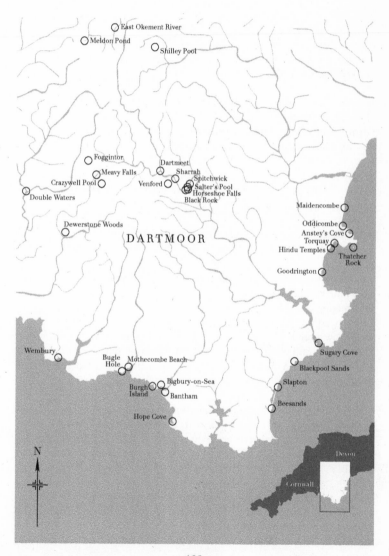

189

ACKNOWLEDGEMENTS

To be entrusted with another writer's work after just one meeting is rare and extraordinary. For that I remain ever grateful to Lynne Roper herself, and her parents Jenny and Mike. I hope Lynne's family members will approve of how I have presented her words.

I would like to thank Emma Pusill for arranging my visit to St Lukes Hospice in Plymouth, and for meeting me there, in the summer of 2016 when Lynne's condition worsened suddenly. She has become a woman I go to for advice on life and book-making both.

Sophie Pierce has not only written movingly of her close friendship with Lynne for the introduction to this book, she has also provided me with annotated maps and much-needed encouragement.

Allan Macfadyen's photographs of Lynne in her element never cease to move me. I thank him for allowing use of them here.

To all of the other swimming companions Lynne writes about in this book, my warmest thanks for entrusting me with photographs, background information and messages of support.

Kate Rew and Kari Furre, directors of the Outdoor Swimming Society and friends of Lynne, greeted my work on these diaries with the kind of warmth and vision they bring to all their art, writing and wild swimming projects.

Jenny Landreth, like me, met Lynne only once – and put her in *Swell: A Waterbiography* on the strength of it. To have an established writer like Jenny support this project has meant a great deal. The long afternoon's talk she and I had beside Pells Pool in the first year of my residency there lasts in memory.

Robert Macfarlane is another established writer to whom I owe thanks. He has been generous in sharing the story of Lynne's life and writing with his large and engaged online following.

That Libby Page agreed to be an early reader and online supporter of this book while her debut novel *The Lido* was newly-arrived in the bestseller lists speaks volumes about her. Thank you, Libby.

I met Ella Chloe Foote only briefly on my visit to Lynne's hospice — she was next in line that day. I have since been lucky enough to be 'swimterviewed' by her for Outdoor Swimmer magazine, and to become then a friend. She has helped me find a far wider audience for Lynne's work than I could have alone.

Jenny Rice spotted the project early on and booked me to share Lynne's story with over three hundred people for the Alpkit Outdoor Swimming Session at the 2017 Kendal Mountain Festival. Many of the audience members there have helped spread word of Lynne's writing online, Louise Barber and Jill Gregory Page chief among them.

Jo Mortimer was the best proofreader for a book of this kind: a nature lover whose passion for language and attention to detail is similar to Lynne's.

My gratitude to Raphael Whittle for gifting his time and skill to bring Lynne's words into print. His own fascination with place matches hers, and is evident in the design of this book.

Finally, heartfelt thanks to my husband Ceri Williams and our children for supporting me in the two years where I have sometimes needed to be more involved in Lynne's life than theirs.

My young daughter left a message on my desk in a difficult week that is precious to me: *'Keep on doing what you are doing and never give up because I and everyone else supports you.'* I did indeed feel the goodwill of all the people mentioned here. Together, we've launched a book that shows in turn our great respect and admiration for Lynne Roper and her wonderful writing.

THE **SELKIE** *PRESS*

www.selkiepress.com